COLIN POWELL

COLIN POWELL

Warren Brown

Senior Consulting Editor
Nathan Irvin Huggins
Director
W.E.B. Du Bois Institute for Afro-American Research
Harvard University

GROLIER INCORPORATED
Danbury, Connecticut

Chelsea House Publishers
Editor-in-Chief Remmel Nunn
Managing Editor Karyn Gullen Browne
Copy Chief Mark Rifkin
Picture Editor Adrian G. Allen
Art Director Maria Epes
Assistant Art Director Howard Brotman
Manufacturing Director Gerald Levine
Systems Manager Lindsey Ottman
Production Manager Joseph Romano
Production Coordinator Marie Claire Cebrián

Black Americans of Achievement
Senior Editor Richard Rennert

Staff for COLIN POWELL
Copy Editor Christopher Duffy
Editorial Assistant Michele Berezansky
Designer Ghila Krajzman
Picture Researcher Lisa Kirchner
Cover Illustration Cynthia Lechan

Published for Grolier by Chelsea House
Copyright © 1990 by Chelsea House Publishers, a division of Main
Line Book Co. All rights reserved. Printed and bound in the United
States of America.

3 5 7 9 8 6 4

Library of Congress Cataloging-in-Publication Data
Brown, Warren
   Colin Powell: military leader/by Warren Brown
   p. cm.—(Black Americans of achievement)
   Includes bibliographical references and index.
Summary: Examines the life and career of the first black chairman
of the Joint Chiefs of Staff, focusing on his role during the Persian
Gulf war.
ISBN 0-7910-1647-1
      0-7910-1648-X (pbk.)
1. Powell, Colin L.—Juvenile literature. 2. Generals—United
States—Biography—Juvenile literature. 3. Afro-American
generals—Biography—Juvenile literature. 4. United States
Army—Biography—Juvenile literature. [1. Powell, Colin L. 2.
Generals. 3. Afro-Americans—Biography. 4. Persian Gulf war, 1991.]
I. Title. II. Series.
E840.5.P68B76 1992   91-22548
355'.0092—dc20   CIP
[B]   AC

Frontispiece: *General Colin L. Powell displays his class portrait in his Pentagon office, surrounded by students from Intermediate School 52, the junior high school he attended in Hunts Point, New York.*

CONTENTS

—— ❦ ——

ON
ACHIEVEMENT

Coretta Scott King

BEFORE YOU BEGIN this book, I hope you will ask yourself what the word *excellence* means to you. I think that it's a question we should all ask, and keep asking as we grow older and change. Because the truest answer to it should never change. When you think of excellence, perhaps you think of success at work; or of becoming wealthy; or meeting the right person, getting married, and having a good family life.

Those important goals are worth striving for, but there is a better way to look at excellence. As Martin Luther King, Jr., said in one of his last sermons, "I want you to be first in love. I want you to be first in moral excellence. I want you to be first in generosity. If you want to be important, wonderful. If you want to be great, wonderful. But recognize that he who is greatest among you shall be your servant."

My husband, Martin Luther King, Jr., knew that the true meaning of achievement is service. When I met him, in 1952, he was already ordained as a Baptist preacher and was working toward a doctoral degree at Boston University. I was studying at the New England Conservatory and dreamed of accomplishments in music. We married a year later, and after I graduated the following year we moved to Montgomery, Alabama. We didn't know it then, but our notions of achievement were about to undergo a dramatic change.

You may have read or heard about what happened next. What began with the boycott of a local bus line grew into a national movement, and by the time he was assassinated in 1968 my husband had fashioned a black movement powerful enough to shatter forever the practice of racial segregation. What you may not have read about is where he got his method for resisting injustice without compromising his religious beliefs.

He adopted the strategy of nonviolence from a man of a different race, who lived in a different country, and even practiced a different religion. The man was Mahatma Gandhi, the great leader of India, who devoted his life to serving humanity in the spirit of love and nonviolence. It was in these principles that Martin discovered his method for social reform. More than anything else, those two principles were the key to his achievements.

This book is about black Americans who served society through the excellence of their achievements. It forms a part of the rich history of black men and women in America—a history of stunning accomplishments in every field of human endeavor, from literature and art to science, industry, education, diplomacy, athletics, jurisprudence, even polar exploration.

Not all of the people in this history had the same ideals, but I think you will find something that all of them had in common. Like Martin Luther King, Jr., they all decided to become "drum majors" and serve humanity. In that principle—whether it was expressed in books, inventions, or song—they found something outside themselves to use as a goal and a guide. Something that showed them a way to serve others, instead of only living for themselves.

Reading the stories of these courageous men and women not only helps us discover the principles that we will use to guide our own lives but also teaches us about our black heritage and about America itself. It is crucial for us to know the heroes and heroines of our history and to realize that the price we paid in our struggle for equality in America was dear. But we must also understand that we have gotten as far as we have partly because America's democratic system and ideals made it possible.

We are still struggling with racism and prejudice. But the great men and women in this series are a tribute to the spirit of our democratic ideals and the system in which they have flourished. And that makes their stories special and worth knowing. ◀▶

COLIN
POWELL

1

"A COMPLETE SOLDIER"

The first black to serve as chairman of the Joint Chiefs of Staff (JCS), Colin Powell is all smiles as he poses with JCS members (from left to right) U.S. Navy admiral Carlisle A. H. Trost, U.S. Air Force general Larry D. Welch, and U.S. Air Force general Robert T. Herres on November 7, 1989. Powell was asked to head the JCS three months earlier, shortly after being promoted to four-star general.

SHORTLY AFTER THREE o'clock on the afternoon of October 3, 1989, in Arlington, Virginia, the doors of the Pentagon, nerve center of the U.S. Department of Defense, swung open to release a steady stream of people into an immense, carefully manicured courtyard. The 20,000 men and women who oversee the global operations of the world's most powerful military force had been ordered by the Pentagon's head, Secretary of Defense Richard B. Cheney, to stop working so they could formally welcome a new person into the Defense Department's chain of command. At 3:30 on this bright fall afternoon, U.S. Army general Colin Luther Powell would officially assume his duties as the 12th chairman of the Joint Chiefs of Staff (JCS) of the U.S. armed forces.

The selection of General Powell to replace Admiral William J. Crowe, Jr., as the nation's highest-ranking military officer represented a landmark event not only for the Pentagon but for the entire American military. Powell had not earned his commission at one of the regular service branch academies, such as the U.S. Military Academy at West Point, New York, or the U.S. Naval Academy at Annapolis, Maryland. He had instead graduated from the Reserve Officers' Training Corps (ROTC) at the City College of New York. At age 52, he would be the youngest person ever to head the JCS.

Departing JCS chairman Admiral William J. Crowe, Jr., is congratulated on September 29, 1989, by his successor during a retirement ceremony at the U.S. Naval Academy in Annapolis, Maryland. Powell became the highest-ranking military officer in the U.S. Department of Defense when he replaced Crowe as JCS chairman.

Far more important, however, Powell had risen from a childhood of poverty to a position of power and influence that no black American had achieved before. He was about to become the first black to head the U.S. military.

At precisely 3:30 P.M., Powell, tall and imposing in a dark green dress uniform, stepped into the courtyard and strode confidently to a podium bearing the Department of Defense seal. The crowd grew quiet as the general, his face framed by a pair of dark-rimmed reading glasses, his chest covered with service decorations, began his acceptance speech. His wife of 27 years, Alma, along with their 3 grown children—Michael, Linda, and Annemarie—stood among the listeners, as did former secretary of defense Frank C. Carlucci, who had taken notice of Powell in the early 1970s and had helped nurture his career.

Powell recognized the importance of his appointment, and his emotionally charged speech showed it. The responsibilities of his new post left him feeling "humbled and proud," he said. "I'm also very mindful today," he continued, "that the period we are entering may be the most historic period in the postwar era. It will be a time of hope, a time of opportunity, a time of anxiety, of instability, of uncertainty, and, yes, a time of risk and danger. But we are not afraid of the future."

Determined to be a firm leader, Powell proceeded to pierce the fog of doubt that had dogged the American military ever since the humiliation of the Vietnam War. "The constant must be to ensure that our armed forces always remain good," he said, "that they always have what is needed to accomplish their mission, that they are never asked to respond to the call of an uncertain trumpet. We owe them, and the nation, and the world no less."

As chairman of the Joint Chiefs of Staff, Powell would be able to make good on this pledge. The JCS chairman is the principal military adviser to the president, the secretary of defense, and the National Security Council (NSC). He is also the leader of the roughly 2 million active-duty and 1.5 million reserve members of the U.S. armed forces. According to the Historical Division of the JCS, the chairman's responsibilities include:

assisting the President and the Secretary of Defense in the strategic direction of the armed forces; preparing strategic and logistics plans and net assessments; providing for the preparation and review of contingency plans; advising the Secretary of Defense on requirements, programs, and budgets; developing doctrine for joint employment of the armed forces; formulating and coordinating policies for the training and education of the armed forces; providing U.S. representation on the United Nations Military Staff Committee; and performing such other duties prescribed by law or by the President and the Secretary of Defense.

The chairman also presides over the JCS meetings and serves as spokesman. All the while, he must be a shrewd politician because it is his duty to maintain a balance of funding and power among the various military branches and to lobby for the military's interests in Congress.

President Franklin D. Roosevelt established the JCS in 1942, one month after the United States entered World War II. Initially, the JCS was the American half of the Combined Chiefs of Staff (CCS), the supreme military body for the joint British-American war effort. The four officers who represented the U.S. military at CCS strategy sessions were formally known as the Joint U.S. Chiefs of Staff. In addition to conferring with their British counterparts, they served as a military advisory committee to the president on the use of armed forces.

The National Security Act of 1947 reorganized the JCS to meet the needs of postwar America. Made up of the heads of the U.S. Army, Navy, and Air Force, the JCS was authorized to provide for the strategic direction of the military forces and to serve as the principal military advisory body to the president and the secretary of defense. The position of chairman, its holder to be nominated by the president and confirmed by the Senate, was created in 1949.

When Powell became chairman, he not only reached an unheard-of position for a black in the

armed forces but had attained it in record time. His list of qualifications was impressive indeed. During his previous 31 years in the army, he had received 2 decorations for valor in the Vietnam War, had held commands in Korea and West Germany, and had served as both the senior military assistant to the secretary of defense and as the National Security Council adviser under President Ronald Reagan. In addition, Powell had been promoted to the army's highest rank, four-star general, four months prior to being nominated to head the JCS. None of the

Secretary of Defense Richard B. Cheney swears the 12th JCS chairman into office on October 3, 1989, at the Pentagon in Arlington, Virginia. Powell's wife, Alma, holds the Bible for her husband as he recites the oath.

The newly sworn-in JCS chairman reviews an honor guard at the October 3, 1989, induction ceremony hosted by Defense Secretary Dick Cheney (left) at the Pentagon. Powell agreed to serve a second term as chairman when his two-year appointment neared its conclusion in 1991.

generals who preceded him as chairman had earned a fourth star faster than Powell had.

On Defense Secretary Cheney's recommendation, President George Bush had selected Powell for the post over 36 more senior officers. "The president wasn't exactly a tough sell," *Newsweek* magazine quoted a White House source as saying. "He thinks the world of Colin." Bush confirmed this sentiment in a speech on August 10, 1989. "Colin Powell has had a truly distinguished military career and he's a complete soldier," the president said. "He will be a key member of my national security team."

Democrat Sam Nunn of Georgia, the chairman of the Senate Armed Services Committee (which must approve any presidential military appointment), agreed with Bush. Nunn remarked upon hearing of Powell's appointment that the general would bring "tremendous . . . talent, insight, and experience" to the position. John Warner of Virginia, the committee's ranking member of the Republican party, echoed the strong feelings of approval for Powell's nomination. "It would have been easy to pick the next most senior officer," Warner commented. "But here, a deep selection was made, which conveys to me [that] some thought went into the decision." The full Senate confirmed Powell's appointment without a single dissenting vote two days after the Armed Services Committee approved his nomination.

Neither the Senate nor the Armed Services Committee made any mention of Powell's race. Yet the choice of a black to fill the nation's highest military position, especially when a conservative Republican administration controlled the White House, could not help but cause some surprise. A friend of Powell's remarked in an interview with *Jet* magazine, "Before this, the only blacks constantly around a U.S. President were valets and the first family servants."

Powell understood as well as anyone that his appointment was of great significance to black America. During much of the nation's history, the U.S. military had excluded blacks from its ranks or had limited them to segregated units under the command of white officers. It had taken many battles on numerous fronts before the military had become an institution that based opportunity on merit rather than race.

Powell was quick to acknowledge that he owed a tremendous debt to the many blacks who had fought to be treated by the U.S. military on equal terms with whites. His new post, he declared to a convention of black journalists shortly after he was nominated as chairman of the JCS, "would not have been possible without the sacrifices of those of our soldiers who served this great nation in war for 300 years previously. . . . All is on the backs and the contributions of those who went before me."

For the most part, though, Powell preferred to look ahead, for he was taking over as chairman of the JCS at a pivotal time in American history. The United States faced unprecedented global changes as its principal adversary in the postwar era, the Soviet Union, released its grip on Eastern Europe and seemed willing to end the cold war. As the warming of relations between the Soviet Union and the United States shifted the focus of global tensions from superpower rivalry to regional threats in the Americas and the Middle East, Congress became more interested in arms control and in reducing the federal budget than in funding a military for tensions that seemed all but over.

As the new chairman of the JCS, it was Powell's responsibility to allocate the money in the military's $290 billion budget and make decisions about the size and role of the U.S. armed forces—decisions that would strongly affect their future. His acceptance speech at the Pentagon indicated that he was prepared for the task. Powell's stirring words left no doubt that he intended to lead the armed services into this new era aggressively. He also clearly intended to help restore public faith in the military's ability to carry out the missions assigned to it.

Powell concluded his Pentagon introduction ceremony by reviewing an assembly of troops in parade formation. The long lines of blue-clad soldiers stood at attention, their rifles resting on the ground and their ceremonial flags waving in the breeze. Their new leader strode firmly in front of this racially mixed group, his posture and expression radiating self-assurance and natural ease with command. That Colin Powell now stood at the pinnacle of American military power spoke volumes about his own abilities—and about how much the armed forces had changed since the time of his birth. ❧

2

"MAKE SOMETHING OF YOUR LIFE"

The future army general at age 15 is flanked by his mother, Maud; sister, Marilyn; and father, Luther. Colin's parents preached to both their children the importance of a good education and personal achievement.

COLIN LUTHER POWELL was born on April 5, 1937, in New York City's Harlem district. Formerly an area of open farmland and country estates, Harlem became a residential neighborhood in the late 19th century, when a mixture of wealthy and working-class whites moved there to escape Manhattan's congested downtown area. To keep pace with the growing demand for housing, real estate developers constructed magnificent town houses and apartment buildings in this uptown section. By 1900, Harlem had emerged as one of the most desirable places to live in the city.

These developers overestimated the demand for housing, however, and by the early 1900s many apartments in Harlem were empty because not enough people could afford to live in such a high-rent district. Desperate to fill the vacant apartments, Harlem landlords drastically lowered their rents. The sudden availability of quality housing attracted large numbers of blacks seeking to escape the racial violence and poor living conditions in the city's congested West Side ghetto, and they moved to Harlem in droves. By the beginning of World War I, 50,000 blacks resided in Harlem and formed a vibrant community with a middle-class standard of living.

Colin's parents, Luther Theopolis Powell and the former Maud Ariel McKoy, arrived in Harlem during the early 1920s, when the community was at its most prosperous. Both parents were from the island of Jamaica and had left their Caribbean homeland in the hope of finding their fortune in the United States. Like so many other immigrants drawn by the booming American economy during the 1920s, they settled in New York City, the thriving metropolis at the mouth of the Hudson River; with its bustling port and enormous wealth, the city seemed to offer limitless opportunity to anyone who sought a better life.

Neither Luther Powell nor Maud McKoy had finished high school, and so they had little choice but to join the large pool of working-class immigrants that served as the backbone of the city's labor force. Luther, a husky young man with a pleasant, round face, found work as a shipping clerk in a garment factory. At a picnic one day in the Bronx, New York City's only mainland borough, he met Maud McKoy. Shortly afterward, the pair married and made their home in Harlem.

Meanwhile, Harlem had begun to take on a special allure. As it became one of the few areas in the country where blacks could enjoy an unusually high quality of life, its writers, musicians, and actors celebrated their racial heritage and promoted their own culture. This awakening of black artistic and intellectual achievement came to be known as the Harlem Renaissance.

Yet underneath the surface of this growing, closely knit community lay the symptoms of decline. By 1930, 200,000 of New York City's 327,000 blacks lived in Harlem, and they were all crowded together in an area that had housed only a quarter of that number 15 years earlier. When the Great Depression began to ravage the nation in the 1930s, Harlem was especially hard hit. Long lines of unemployed people

Young Colin with a few of his friends from the Hunts Point, New York, neighborhood in which he grew up. So many minorities lived there, Powell said later, that he "didn't know what a 'majority' was."

in search of food and clothing stretched in front of the local churches and charity organizations. Families evicted from their apartments because they could not pay the rent crowded into the homes of relatives or lived on the street. What had previously been one of New York City's most beautiful areas began to deteriorate rapidly.

It was into this black community, in desperate decline but still treasuring proud memories, that Colin Powell was born. He lived in Harlem until he was three years old; then his parents decided it was time to relocate. In 1940, Luther and Maud Powell packed their belongings; and with Colin and his sister, Marylin, who was five and a half years older than him, in tow, they followed the city's ever expanding elevated railway line northeast, across the Harlem River to the Bronx.

The Powells settled in Hunts Point, a working-class neighborhood in the southeastern section of the borough. The family made its home in a walk-up apartment building on Kelly Street. In time, the area would reach the extreme levels of urban decay and devastation that have come to characterize Harlem. But in the 1940s, residents called the borough "the beautiful Bronx," and Harlemites who moved into Hunts Point's blue-collar neighborhood felt that they had moved up in the world.

Although the local population was mainly Jewish, Hunts Point contained a mixture of New York City's various immigrant groups. Jews mixed freely with blacks, Irish, Italians, Poles, and Puerto Ricans, and their children mingled unselfconsciously in play. As a result, young Colin never paid much attention to the color of his skin. "I grew up in a neighborhood where everybody was a minority," he recalled. "I never thought there was something wrong with me because I was black."

The fact that his parents came from Jamaica also contributed to Colin's lack of self-consciousness about his race. Even though blacks in Jamaica were British subjects, they rarely experienced the sort of racial oppression that many black Americans, particularly those in the southern states, endured. When Powell's parents arrived in the United States, they did not view themselves as second-class citizens, and they never allowed their children to think that way either.

Instead, Luther and Maud Powell instilled in their son and daughter a strong faith in the Anglican church and a healthy respect for formal education. They wanted Colin and Marylin to do well in life and insisted that getting ahead in America depended on learning as much as possible. As a result, the Powell children often received lectures from their parents to "strive for a good education. Make something of your life."

Luther and Maud Powell also told their children that only hard work and perseverance could lead to success. Colin recalled later, "There was something of a tradition of hard work being the way to succeed, and there was simply an expectation that existed in the family—you were supposed to do better. And it was a bloody disappointment to the family if you didn't."

Colin's parents certainly led by example. Each morning, Luther Powell left home at an early hour to catch the elevated train to his job in New York City's Garment District, and he remained there all day, never returning home from work until at least 7:00 or 8:00 in the evening. Maud Powell found a job as a seamstress, and she too spent many long hours doing her work. "It wasn't a matter of spending a great deal of time with my parents discussing things," Colin remembered. "We didn't sit down at night . . . and review the work of the day. It was just the way they lived their lives."

Even though both his parents worked, young Colin never went unsupervised during the day. Maud's mother, who was known to everyone as Miss Alice, and other relatives stayed with him and his sister to enforce discipline. In addition, nearby families made a habit of watching one another's children. Marylin recalled years later that "when you walked down the street, you had all these eyes watching you."

In spite of this upbringing, Colin showed few signs during his childhood of responding to his parents' desire that he apply himself in school. Early on in elementary school, when he was about eight years old, he attempted to play hooky. The young truant estimated the time wrong, however, and arrived

At Morris High School in the South Bronx, Powell lettered in track and was elected class representative. He also served as treasurer of the Service League (above), a group that performed helpful deeds at the school.

home too early. A family friend caught him, and a family discussion ensued. In the days that followed, an adult was always present to take Colin by the hand and lead him to the classroom door.

Colin, however, did not change his ways. As a fifth grader at Public School 39, he was such a lackluster student that he landed in the slow class. At both Intermediate School 52 and Morris High School, he continued to apply himself indifferently. In his own words, he "horsed around a lot" and managed to keep his grades only barely above passing. His unspectacular marks kept him from realizing an ambition to attend the Bronx High School of Science, one of the nation's finest schools.

By this time, Colin had developed into a tall, strong teenager with a natural flair for leadership. At Morris High School, he was elected class representative, served as treasurer of the Service League, whose members helped out around the school, and lettered in track. Neighborhood youths learned not to push him around. He moved freely among Hunts Point's various racial groups and even managed to learn some Yiddish while working after school at Sickser's, a store that sold baby furniture. In his free time, Colin and his best friend, Gene Norman, raced bicycles along the sweeping curve of Kelly Street or played games of stickball.

When Colin graduated from Morris High School in early 1954, he said that he wanted to become an engineer; but in reality, he had very little idea of what he wanted to do with his life. His parents, insisting that he lift himself out of Hunts Point's "$40-a-week, lower blue-collar environment," made it clear that they expected him to go to college. Colin had no particular urge to get a higher education, but he had a deeply ingrained sense of obedience to his mother and father. If they expected him to attend college, he would go.

Colin applied to New York University and to the City College of New York. Despite his low grades, both institutions accepted him. Tuition costs helped Colin narrow down his choice. New York University charged students $750 per year to attend. The City College of New York, situated on 138th Street in upper Manhattan, enrolled any graduate from a New York City high school for only a token $10 fee. Accordingly, on a cold winter day in February 1954, Colin took a bus to Manhattan and began his life as a City College student.

Colin enrolled in City College's engineering program, and he did moderately well at first, ending his initial semester with a B average. But during the summer of 1954, he took a mechanical drawing course, and it proved to be the most miserable summer of his life. When, on a boiling hot afternoon,

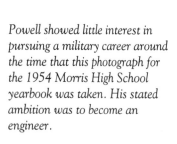

Powell showed little interest in pursuing a military career around the time that this photograph for the 1954 Morris High School yearbook was taken. His stated ambition was to become an engineer.

his instructor asked him to imagine a cone intersecting a plane in space, Colin decided that he had had enough of engineering and dropped out of the program.

Colin decided to change his major to geology, not because of any strong interest in the subject but because he thought it would be easy. He did not push himself very hard and saw his average creep down to a C.

Nevertheless, Colin was about to display his first real enthusiasm for a school-related activity. During his first spring at City College, he had noticed uniformed members of the Army Reserve Officers'

Training Corps walking around the campus. The ROTC offered students military training that could lead to a commission as an officer in the U.S. Army. Colin decided that he liked the serious look of the members of the Pershing Rifles, the ROTC drill team, who wore small whipped cords on their uniform shoulders.

Colin already possessed a mild interest in the military. In high school, he had closely followed the unfolding of the Korean War. His interest aroused, Colin signed up for the ROTC for the fall semester of 1954 and pledged himself to the Pershing Rifles.

At that point, Colin had no intention of making the army a career. He wanted only to find a way to escape from New York City for a while and, in his own words, "have some excitement." Besides, joining the ROTC would help him find work. He expected to serve no more than two years in the army after graduating from college "and then come home and get a real job." But as it turned out, he had stumbled onto his life's calling.

3

BUFFALO SOLDIERS

WHEN COLIN POWELL entered City College's ROTC program in the fall of 1954, he was taking advantage of an opportunity that was relatively new to black Americans. The U.S. Army and its officer training programs had not always welcomed blacks with open arms. Even though black soldiers had displayed their skill and heroism countless times during the nation's wars, the United States refused to desegregate its armed forces until 1948.

The U.S. military's long history of discriminating against blacks began with the first settlers. As these colonists established their homes along North America's eastern coast during the late 17th and early 18th centuries, they formed local militias to protect themselves from hostile Native Americans. Every able-bodied man who could shoulder a musket—a description that included many freed blacks and slaves—served the community during an emergency.

As the slave trade grew and America's colonial leaders began to fear that slaves would turn their weapons on their white masters, laws were formed to bar blacks from serving in the militia. Virginia

Troop E of the Ninth U.S. Cavalry assembles for a group portrait en route to the Philippines in 1900. One of the first all-black combat regiments, the Ninth Cavalry was originally stationed in the Old West, where its members became known as the Buffalo Soldiers.

One of the 185,000 blacks who served with distinction in the Civil War, drummer boy Jackson (above, right) stands proudly in full uniform, a vast improvement over the rags he wore (above, left) before enlisting in the Union army. Shortly after the war, the federal government established the regular army's first all-black regiments, thereby opening a door of opportunity for blacks who wanted a career in the military.

enacted the first such law in 1639; Massachusetts instituted similar legislation in 1656. Hartford, Connecticut, followed suit in 1661 after blacks and Native Americans in the area attempted a revolt.

By the middle of the 18th century, blacks throughout the colonies were allowed to serve in militias only as laborers, cooks, musicians, and in other noncombat roles. Still, from time to time there arose emergencies in which it became necessary for whites to allow blacks to join them on the firing line. In 1715, for example, North Carolina whites armed their slaves to help turn aside an attack by the Yamasee and Creek Indians. Most whites did not feel very comfortable with this solution. "There must be great caution used," one of them said on the subject of distributing weapons to blacks, "lest our slaves when arm'd become our masters."

Among those who agreed with this view was George Washington, who commanded the patriots' forces, the Continental army, during the American Revolution. In October 1775, half a year after British troops clashed with the patriot militia for the first time, he banned all blacks from enlisting in the Continental army. It was not until the following year, after the British formally invited free blacks and slaves to join their side, that Washington, facing a critical shortage of manpower, permitted blacks to fight alongside whites.

By the time the American Revolution ended in 1783, about 5,000 blacks had served in the revolutionary forces. They had proven extremely capable and dedicated, yet the mistrust that whites felt toward armed blacks quickly reasserted itself. In 1792, Congress passed a law limiting the recruitment of state militias to white men between the ages of 18 and 45. Most states interpreted the new law as a total ban on black enrollment.

Nevertheless, in the 19th century—as in colonial times—necessity prompted white military leaders to bend the law by drawing on the black population for manpower. Hastily formed black militia units helped fight British forces in the War of 1812. Half a century later, a shortage of white volunteers during the Civil War forced Northern generals to form black regiments without official permission. President Abraham Lincoln had expressly prohibited blacks from serving in the Union army because he feared it would anger most of the white soldiers and cause tension in the ranks. He also felt that allowing blacks to fight the Confederacy might jeopardize the allegiance of the few slaveholding states that had remained loyal to the Union.

In 1879, Henry Flipper became the first black to graduate from the U.S. Military Academy at West Point, New York. It took another 69 years, however, for the armed forces to become fully integrated.

As the Civil War dragged on, Massachusetts governor John Andrews declared that Northerners no longer cared whether their soldiers traced their roots "from the banks of the Thames or the banks of the Senegal." The Union simply needed more troops. Lincoln agreed that more soldiers were needed, and in 1862 he authorized the arming and training of blacks. By the end of the war, the U.S. Bureau of Colored Troops had recruited and trained more than 185,000 black soldiers.

Despite this large number, blacks constantly faced discrimination in the Union army. They were assigned to segregated units under the command of whites and were given menial tasks to perform. On those occasions when they were allowed to fight alongside whites, they displayed the same degree of courage that their ancestors had shown in earlier wars. The most celebrated black Civil War unit was one of the first: the 54th Massachusetts Regiment, which spearheaded an unsuccessful assault on a Confederate fort in South Carolina. Led by a young white colonel named Robert Gould Shaw, the 54th lost more than half its men during an attempt to capture Fort Wagner. All told, more than 38,000 black soldiers died in the Civil War.

After the war ended, Congress awarded blacks a permanent place in the army. Four all-black regiments were formed: the 24th and 25th Infantry regiments and the Ninth and 10th Cavalry regiments. As with the black regiments established during the Civil War, white officers led these units. Federal officials instituted one other significant measure: They stationed all four regiments out west to remove them from public view. The Native Americans in the western territories likened the short, curly hair and the stamina of these men to the plains buffalo's and christened them the Buffalo Soldiers.

The Buffalo Soldiers soon showed that they were excellent fighters, yet the army still treated them like outcasts. During the Spanish-American War in 1898, the Ninth and 10th Cavalry regiments were sent to Cuba but had to fight on foot because they were not supplied with horses. Both regiments helped ensure an American victory in the pivotal battle at San Juan Hill, although neither one received much credit for its effort. Soon-to-be-president Theodore Roosevelt and his white Rough Riders, who also participated in the battle, downplayed the Buffalo Soldiers' contribution and claimed the lion's share of the victory for themselves.

Discrimination toward black soldiers showed itself once again in 1906, when a riot broke out in

Brownsville, Texas, and the men of the 25th Infantry, stationed on the edge of town, were accused of starting the violence. Even though there was no clear-cut evidence against the black troops, President Theodore Roosevelt called for three entire companies to be dishonorably discharged from the army. As a result, 167 soldiers, some with up to 27 years of military service and several having already been awarded the Congressional Medal of Honor, were booted out of the army. None of them received any pension, benefits, or back pay, let alone any official recognition of their past service.

Despite these incidents, a few blacks began to make headway in the army's hierarchy. In 1879, Henry Flipper became the first black to graduate from the U.S. Military Academy at West Point. Ten years later, Charles Young, the third black to graduate from the academy, took his military career a few steps further. By the end of World War I, he had become a high-ranking officer.

After he left West Point, Young taught military science at Wilberforce University, commanded the Ninth Cavalry during the Spanish-American War, and served as military attaché to both Haiti and Liberia. In 1916, he headed a squadron of the 10th Cavalry and helped General John ("Black Jack") Pershing pursue the Mexican revolutionary Pancho Villa. Young's heroics during this campaign earned him the rank of lieutenant colonel.

But even Young was a victim of discrimination. By the start of World War I, he seemed poised to become the nation's first black general. In 1917, however, army physicians blocked his promotion by declaring the 53-year-old officer physically unfit for active duty. Outraged, Young proved his fitness by riding the 500 miles from his Ohio home to Washington, D.C., on horseback. Still, army doctors refused to reinstate him. He was kept out of the

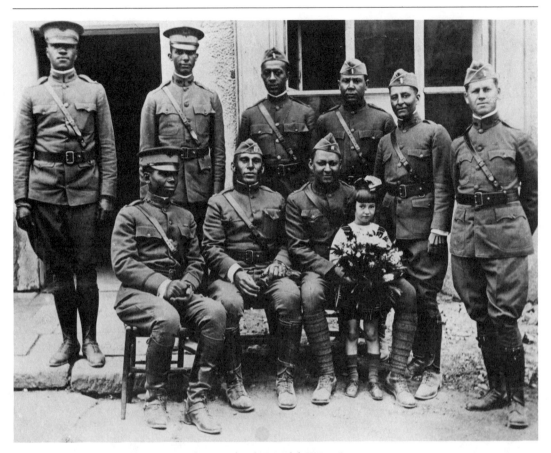

service until shortly before the end of World War I. By that time, all chance of his being promoted to general had passed.

The army's treatment of Young during World War I exemplified its handling of black soldiers, most of whom ended up serving as laborers. Those who were sent into combat had to contend with inadequate training, poor equipment, and unenthusiastic white commanders. They were also barred from using the same facilities as whites.

Prior to the war, blacks had hoped their participation in the conflict would earn them greater respect from white America. Instead, they continued to face discriminatory treatment. Of the 370,000 blacks who served in the military during World War I, only 5

Black officers were a rarity in World War I, as the armed forces averaged 1 black officer per every 2,600 black soldiers. None of the black officers, including these members of the 367th Infantry, 77th Division, held a rank higher than colonel.

held officers' commissions in the army; none held a commission in the air corps.

By the time Colin Powell was born, the situation had hardly improved; indeed, the army showed little desire to end segregation in its ranks. It was not until 1940, when the United States was preparing to enter World War II, that a few of the barriers finally began to crumble. The military established several black combat units and officer candidate schools for the training of blacks as combat pilots. Moreover, Benjamin O. Davis, Sr., broke new ground when he was named the nation's first black general. The army, however, refused to renounce its policy of segregation or to stop relegating black recruits to service units.

When given the opportunity, black troops served with distinction. The 92nd Infantry Division, nicknamed the Buffalo Division after the black troops who had fought in the American West, won 65 Silver Stars, 162 Bronze Stars, and 1,300 Purple Hearts. The all-black 332nd Fighter Group, commanded by Col-

Benjamin O. Davis, Sr. (below, right), and his son, Benjamin O. Davis, Jr. (below, left), were among the first blacks to rise to the top of the military. In 1940, the army promoted the senior Davis to brigadier general—the first black American to attain such a high rank. Fourteen years later, the junior Davis became the first black general in the air force.

onel Benjamin O. Davis, Jr., son of the first black general, destroyed 260 enemy planes and damaged 148 others in 1,579 missions. Its pilots were awarded more than 800 medals.

In light of such gallant efforts, criticism of the army's segregation policy grew stronger during the mid-1940s. A. Philip Randolph, Walter White, and other black leaders stepped up their campaign to desegregate the armed forces. Finally, in July 1948, President Harry S. Truman gave in to the demands and issued two landmark executive orders: He desegregated the armed forces and called for government agencies to institute fair employment practices. The door for equal opportunity had begun to open for Colin Powell and other black Americans. ◆

U.S. armed forces remained racially segregated until 1948, when President Harry S. Truman ordered an end to discrimination in the military "as rapidly as possible." By the time the Korean War began two years later, most combat troops, including the Second Infantry Division (above), had become integrated.

4

"HEY, THIS IS FUN!"

While attending City College of New York, Powell became commander of the Pershing Rifles, the Reserve Officers' Training Corps (ROTC) precision drill team; he also served as president of the Cadet Officers' Club and graduated at the top of his ROTC class. "There was no specific point," he later said of his decision to make the army his career. "I just never found or saw anything I liked better."

THE SAME YEAR that Colin Powell enrolled in City College's ROTC program, the Pentagon announced that the army had become totally desegregated. Blacks who entered the military in 1954 would find their chances for advancement limited only by their ability. And no recruit would make more of this newly won opportunity than Powell.

It dawned on the teenager right away that military life suited him. He liked the physical activity and the discipline that the ROTC program demanded of him. He also enjoyed the camaraderie he felt among the members of the Pershing Rifles as they went through their drills in New York City's 369th Armory. As a result, he did not bring the same carefree attitude to the ROTC program that he did to other courses. For the first time ever, he received A's for his work. "Hey, this is fun!" Powell said of the ROTC in his sophomore year. He had at last found a pursuit that appealed to him.

One of the things the ROTC did for Powell was to give him his first look at black life in other parts of the United States. A few months after he turned 19 years old, he enrolled in a training program at Fort Bragg, North Carolina, for the summer. His father saw him off from New York City, unsure how Colin would survive his first encounter with southern racism. In the South, Jim Crow laws (a term that originated in the popular blackface minstrel shows of the late 19th and early 20th centuries) gave racial prejudice full legal backing by restricting black access in public accommodations.

Jim Crow laws assigned blacks to inferior schools and hospitals and demanded that they use separate restaurants, drinking fountains, toilets, and waiting rooms. These laws also required separate seating sections for blacks in the rear of buses, trains, and movie theaters and banned them from using city parks and beaches. All told, Jim Crow laws touched on practically every aspect of black southern life.

Powell's upbringing in Hunts Point's racial melting pot had not prepared him for the antiblack attitudes he encountered in North Carolina. "It was only [when I arrived]," he said later, "that I had brought home to me in stunning clarity the way things were in other parts of the United States." By the time the summer was over, he had become much more determined to make something of himself.

This new outlook revealed itself after Powell returned to City College. He encouraged his ROTC classmates to work harder and was appointed head of the Pershing Rifles. During his senior year, he attained the ROTC's highest rank, cadet colonel. And by the time he graduated from City College in 1958, he stood at the top of his ROTC class.

After graduation, Powell was commissioned as a second lieutenant in the army and received a weekly salary of $60. Despite his strong showing in the ROTC program, he did not have very great expectations for his future. No black American had ever risen higher than the rank of brigadier, or one-star, general. "If you do everything well and keep your nose clean for 20 years," his superiors told him, "we'll make you a lieutenant colonel." Powell set his sights on meeting that goal. A career officer with 20 years of service was eligible to retire from the military with a full pension, which meant solid financial security to a son of immigrant parents.

Second Lieutenant Powell embarked on the typical nomadic life of a young army officer. He went first to Fort Benning, Georgia, the home of the army's Infantry School. There he took courses in airborne infantry and attended classes for the small commando units, known as Rangers, that specialized in surprise raids.

After completing his training in Georgia, Powell shipped out for West Germany, where he joined other U.S. soldiers in maintaining a watch on the troops of the Warsaw Pact nations. He served first as a platoon leader, then became the commander of a rifle company. By the time Powell returned to the United States in 1960, he was a first lieutenant. His climb up the military's ladder of success had begun.

Indeed, the 24-year-old first lieutenant had already managed to make a favorable impression on his superiors. The army assigned him to take over as battalion adjutant in an infantry battalion stationed at Fort Devens, Massachusetts. Normally, this post was assigned to a higher-ranking officer than a first lieutenant—usually, to a captain—and brought with it responsibility for all decisions regarding the battalion's personnel.

(The smallest unit in the U.S. Army is a *squad*, which comprises 5 to 10 soldiers and is commanded by a noncommissioned officer, usually a sergeant. A group of several squads, amounting to 30 to 50 soldiers, is called a *platoon*; it is most often headed by a lieutenant. Three to four platoons form a *company*, which is usually led by a captain. Three to five companies make up a *battalion*, which is generally overseen by a lieutenant colonel.)

From December 1962 to November 1963, First Lieutenant Powell was stationed in Vietnam (above and opposite page), where he served as military adviser to a South Vietnamese infantry battalion. He returned to Southeast Asia in June 1968 for a second tour of duty, this time as an infantry battalion executive officer and assistant chief of staff, and he continued to see action in the Vietnam War until July 1969.

Powell's natural ease with people made him well suited for his new job as battalion adjutant. His commanding officer, Colonel William Abernathy, taught him the ropes. Powell later declared that he "learned a lot from Bill Abernathy about how to treat soldiers." In turn, Powell struck the colonel as "wise beyond his years" in dealing with problems of discipline and morale, perhaps because Powell himself had not always been especially motivated. In any event, the first lieutenant "performed magnificently," Abernathy said later. "He was always thinking and planning ahead."

Powell was still stationed in Massachusetts in 1962 when he went on a blind date while on leave in Boston. His companion for the evening was Alma

Johnson, an attractive young speech pathologist from Birmingham, Alabama. "He was absolutely the nicest person I had ever met," she recalled. He also seemed different from most other servicemen. When Alma asked him when he would be getting out of the army, he replied that he intended making it a career. "Everyone else I knew in the army," Alma said later, "had the days and minutes of their remaining service counted."

Favorably impressed, Alma Johnson agreed to see Powell again and again over the next few months. During the summer, the couple decided to wed, even though Powell had received word he would be leaving the States by year's end for reassignment in Southeast Asia. They were married on August 25, 1962.

At the end of 1962, Powell took leave of his wife to join the rapidly growing American military force in Vietnam. Since the mid-1950s, the United States had been helping to bolster the South Vietnamese government against attacks by the Communist rebels of North Vietnam. But by the early 1960s, the South

Vietnamese government had become so endangered that President John F. Kennedy sent thousands of American military personnel, under the guise of advisers, to fight alongside the South Vietnamese troops. Powell's assignment was to serve as an adviser to a South Vietnamese infantry battalion patrolling the jungles along the Laos border.

By the spring of 1963, Powell was leading a combat unit near the North Vietnamese border. There he received word that Alma, who had moved to Birmingham to live with her parents while her husband was stationed overseas, had given birth to a boy, Michael. More than half a year would pass before Powell's tour of duty ended and he could return to the States to see his first child.

One day that summer, Powell and his men were wading through a Vietnamese rice-paddy field when he stepped on an enemy trap, a sharpened stake (known as a punji stick) that had been concealed just below the surface of the water. Powell impaled his left foot on the stake with such force that it came out the top of his boot. The army shipped him to the nearby coastal city of Hue to treat his wound. He returned to the jungle a few weeks later with his first combat decoration, the Purple Heart, to show for his injury.

While Powell was braving the dangers of Vietnam, his wife was in the middle of a different kind of battle. Her hometown of Birmingham had a well-deserved reputation as being the most segregated city in the South. With that in mind, Martin Luther King, Jr., and other black leaders decided to make Birmingham a focal point of the civil rights movement. "We knew that as Birmingham went, so would go the South," said a King aide, Wyatt T. Walker. "And we felt that if we could crack that city, then we could crack any city."

Powell takes a break outside his barracks during his second tour of duty in Vietnam. The lessons he learned from the Vietnam War led him to conclude that an army should not enter into combat unless it had a clear objective. "If you finally decide you have to commit military force," he said, "you've got to be as massive and decisive as possible. Decide your target, decide your objective, and try to overwhelm it."

The showdown in Birmingham came to a head in early May 1963, when more than a thousand youngsters took part in a massive civil rights demonstration organized by King. The Birmingham city government responded with a brutal show of force. Birmingham's public safety commissioner, T. Eugene ("Bull") Connor, ordered his men not only to arrest the protesters but to repulse them. Scores of firemen employed high-pressure water hoses to repel the demonstators, slamming them to the ground and knocking them senseless. Mobs of policemen unleashed German shepherd attack dogs and looked the other way as angry whites brutally beat some of the marchers.

Alma's father, J. C. Johnson, who had been a principal in one of the city's all-black high schools, brought home stories of the racial violence. As the tumult reached its peak, he watched over his wife, his daughter, and her infant son, Michael, with a shotgun.

Powell arrived in Birmingham that Christmas, having recently won a Bronze Star for heroism in addition to his Purple Heart. The realization that he had risked his life for his country while his family's safety had been threatened by city officials left him enraged. "I was hit full force with what had happened in my absence," he recalled. "I was stunned, disheartened, and angry." Thereafter, he became a solid supporter of the civil rights movement.

Powell felt the sting of southern racism firsthand after he received orders to leave Birmingham and report once again to Fort Benning. One day, when he was trying to find a house in the area so his wife and son could join him in Georgia, he stopped at a restaurant for a hamburger. The waitress asked Powell if he was a student from Africa. When Powell told her no, the woman asked him, "A Puerto Rican?"

"No," Powell answered.

"You're Negro?"

"That's right."

"Well," the waitress responded, "I can't bring out a hamburger. You'll have to go to the back door."

Powell made a point of returning to the restaurant after President Lyndon B. Johnson signed the Civil Rights Act of 1964 into law on July 2. Among other measures, this law prohibited segregation in public facilities and forbade employers from practicing racial discrimination. "Then I went back to the restaurant," Powell recalled, "and got my hamburger."

That same year, Powell requested and received permission to attend the army's Command and General Staff College at Fort Leavenworth, Kansas— he had not forgotten his parents' lectures about the

Powell freed himself from this wreckage after a helicopter in which he was riding crashed in a Vietnamese jungle. He then pulled a GI from the burning craft—an act of bravery that subsequently earned him the Soldier's Medal.

value of a good education. Meanwhile, Powell himself was becoming a parent once again. In 1965, while he was still stationed in Kansas, his wife gave birth to their second child, Linda. Another daughter, Anne-marie, was born to the Powells in 1971.

Halfway through his Leavenworth course work, Powell asked the army to let him attend a civilian graduate school and add a master's degree to his City College degree in geology. "Your college record isn't good enough," the officer in charge responded. Angrily, Powell buckled down and graduated from Leavenworth second in a class of 1,244. Despite his efforts to prove he was "good enough," Powell did not receive permission to enter a program of graduate study. Instead, the army sent him back to Vietnam.

American involvement in Vietnam had gradually been escalating, and by 1968 it had turned into overt military action. Furthermore, in an increasingly desperate attempt to protect the South Vietnamese regime, the U.S government had progressively raised the number of troops it sent to Vietnam. By June 1968, when Powell joined the American forces in Vietnam as an infantry battalion executive officer and assistant chief of staff with the 23rd Infantry Division, he was one of more than 500,000 servicemen stationed there. He watched with increasing skepticism as the American troops failed to bring the war to a successful close despite their advanced technological weapons and high-powered aircraft.

Shortly after Powell arrived in Vietnam, a stroke of luck pulled him out of constant combat duty in the jungle and placed him on the road to high command. The *Army Times* had just published a story about the year's top five Leavenworth graduates, and the article had caught the eye of the commander of the 23rd Infantry. "I've got the number two Leavenworth graduate in my division, and he's stuck in the boonies?" he shouted at his subordinates. "I want him on my staff!" Powell thus became the division's assistant chief of staff.

From time to time, Powell still went out on combat missions. On one occasion, he accompanied a helicopter unit into the jungle. The pilot tried to set down the craft in a small clearing, but a rotor blade struck a tree and the helicopter crashed. Before the fuel tanks could explode, Powell pulled the pilot from the burning wreckage, a feat that earned him the Soldier's Medal, awarded for voluntarily risking one's life in a noncombat situation.

Powell's second Vietnam tour ended in July 1969. Upon returning to the States, he received permission to continue his education. That fall, he began work on a Master of Business Administration (MBA) degree at George Washington University in Washington, D.C. His reason for pursuing an MBA was quite simple. "Good business managers," he explained years later, "are needed in the Department of Defense." ◉

5

THE CORRIDORS OF POWER

❦

O N JULY 9, 1970, 12 years after he first received a commission in the U.S. Army, Colin Powell was promoted to lieutenant colonel, the rank he had been told it would take him 20 years to attain. The 33-year-old officer now had a guaranteed retirement pension, which gave him and his family a growing sense of security. The following year, he graduated from George Washington University with an MBA. His future seemed secure, whether or not he chose to remain in the army.

In 1972, a stroke of fate similar to the one that had placed him on the 23rd Infantry Division staff landed Powell his first political appointment. He was working as a research analyst in the office of the vice-chief of staff at the Pentagon when he received a phone call from the army's personnel department. "Colin," the caller said, "the Infantry Branch wants one of its people to become a White House Fellow. We want you to apply."

The White House Fellowship program sponsors promising military officers to serve for one year as an assistant in various departments of the executive

In September 1973, Lieutenant Colonel Powell arrived in South Korea to command the First Battalion of the Second Infantry Division's 32nd Infantry Regiment. He resumed his climb up the federal government ladder the following year, when the army rotated him back to the United States and he took a staff job at the Pentagon.

branch. This internship is highly coveted because it grooms talented officers for a role in government policy-making. Powell agreed to apply for a fellowship.

His interview was conducted by Frank Carlucci, a small, wiry deputy secretary from the Office of Management and Budget (OMB). A former foreign service official who had won a State Department medal for rescuing a group of Americans from an angry mob in what is now Zaire, Carlucci took an immediate liking to the lieutenant colonel. Powell received word shortly after the interview that of the more than 1,500 applicants for the fellowship, he was 1 of the 7 people chosen to become a White House Fellow.

Powell's good fortune did not end there. Carlucci invited him to serve as his assistant at the all-important OMB. In effect, the OMB oversees the operations of the executive branch. The OMB helps the president put together the nation's budget for each fiscal year, controls the administration of the budget after Congress has approved it, and provides the president with information on the performance of each government program. Thus, Powell's new assignment not only involved him in the fiscal planning of the executive branch but also gave him a broad view of how it worked. He felt that he had landed what he termed a "dream job."

Along with assisting Carlucci, Powell worked with Carlucci's boss, OMB director Caspar W. Weinberger, who had recently been appointed to the post by President Richard M. Nixon. A tough-minded politician, Cap Weinberger displayed such a willingness to streamline federal finances that he was given the nickname Cap the Knife.

Powell's stint at the OMB proved a turning point in his life. His ability to carry out tasks with extreme competence and little fuss made a lasting impression

on both Carlucci and Weinberger, each of whom was a rising star in Washington politics. Because of their support, Powell would always find the corridors of power open to him in the years that followed.

After Powell's term as a White House Fellow expired in 1973, the army sent him to South Korea in September to take command of the First Battalion of the Second Infantry Division's 32nd Infantry Regiment. Racial tension and a growing drug problem within the regiment had expanded into a major problem. The army was looking for Powell to smooth out the problems and restore a sense of discipline.

Powell quickly displayed the forceful command style that would become his hallmark. He discharged the malcontents—"bums," he later called them—and ordered the drug users put in jail. He ran everyone else four miles each morning and spent the rest of the day working them equally hard; by nightfall, no one

Battalion Commander Powell meets with his junior officers in Korea. He has since attributed his rise in the military to his belief that "there are no secrets to success; don't waste time looking for them. Success is the result of perfection, hard work, learning from failure, loyalty to those for whom you work, and persistence."

Located at Fort Lesley J. McNair in Washington, D.C., the National War College offers a course of study that emphasizes the planning and implementing of national security policy. Powell enrolled there in 1975 and graduated from the college with distinction in late 1976.

had enough energy left to cause trouble. All the while, he emphasized a spirit of cooperation. Within a few months, Powell's approach had yielded clear-cut results. Blacks and whites worked together peacefully and socialized with one another as well.

In 1974, Powell returned to the Pentagon, this time as an operations research analyst in the office of the assistant defense secretary. The army, however, apparently had greater things in store for him. The next year, Powell received word that he had been accepted into the National War College at Fort Lesley J. McNair in the nation's capital.

Founded by the Joint Chiefs of Staff in 1946 to promote understanding among the various branches of the armed forces and to bridge any communications gap between the Defense and State departments, the National War College has since evolved into an institution that provides education in national security policy to selected military officers and career civil service employees of federal departments and agencies concerned with national security. The 10-month academic program emphasizes the study of major issues likely to affect the national security of the United States.

In 1975, Powell, along with nearly 100 officers of comparable rank from the various armed forces and about 40 civilians, began his studies at the National War College. The curriculum would round out his knowledge of the armed forces and their role in national security policy. His course work would also help him learn how to plan and implement national strategy.

In February 1976, while he was still enrolled at the National War College, Powell received a promotion to full colonel. Two months later, partway through his second semester at the college, his superiors pulled him out of school and gave him another field command. He was made brigade commander of the 101st Airborne Division, based at Fort Campbell, Kentucky.

Powell's appointment to the division's Second Brigade brought with it a large measure of prestige. The 101st had fought with distinction during World War II and, along with the 82nd Airborne Division, now made up the army's entire mobile attack force. If the army needed to respond quickly to a military crisis, Powell could almost certainly expect to find himself in the thick of the action.

During his tenure as commander of the Second Brigade, Powell once again showed himself to be a hard-driving, energetic leader. But when the opportunity arose, he revealed another side of his character. A battalion commander in Powell's unit, Lieutenant Colonel Vic Michael, hurt his back after he slipped and fell while getting out of a helicopter. Michael tried to shrug off the injury, but Powell sent him to a doctor. The physician found that spinal surgery was needed to repair the injury.

Powell refused to follow normal army procedures, which would have resulted in another officer assuming command of Michael's battalion. Instead, he helped Michael's junior officers run the battalion and kept the position open until Michael underwent surgery and was healthy enough to resume his duties. "Powell could have ended my career, but he had faith in me," Michael said later. "He acted like he owed me something. I will never forget his understanding for me as a soldier and a human being."

Powell graduated with distinction from the National War College in late 1976. The following summer, after serving as brigade commander for a little more than a year, he returned to the Pentagon as a military assistant in the office of the deputy defense secretary. During his previous postings in Washington, he had served under Republican administrations, first Nixon's and then Gerald Ford's.

Now, a Democrat, Jimmy Carter, sat in the White House, which meant that Powell was working for another Democrat, Deputy Secretary of Defense Charles W. Duncan, Jr.

The change in the political climate made no difference in the way the Pentagon's top brass perceived Powell. He had not been labeled a Republican or a Democrat (in actuality, he considered himself an independent) because he had never shown any leanings toward either of the nation's two main political parties. First and foremost, he was a military officer, and as such he preferred to leave politics to others and perform his duties regardless of which party the national elections had placed in control of the Pentagon.

Powell remained at the Pentagon until 1979, when he briefly went to work at the newly established Department of Energy. His immediate boss at the Defense Department had just been named the new secretary of energy and had invited Powell to come along. "I went to the Department of Energy with him for two to three months," Powell later said of Duncan, "to help him get set up."

Duncan, in turn, took the colonel under his wing and taught him how to achieve his goals in the maze of federal bureaucracy without ruffling any feathers. One of Duncan's rules of thumb, Powell now jokes, stuck with him for life. "When I told [Duncan] something awful had happened," Powell recalled, "he said, 'Well, Colin, if all else fails and we have no choice, tell the truth.'"

In the summer of 1979, at age 42, Powell reached yet another milestone in his military career. On June 1, the army promoted him to brigadier general. When he pinned the general's star on his uniform, he joined the small but growing number of blacks who had risen through their own hard work and merit to such a high rank. He had now achieved much more than he ever thought possible when he had decided to pursue a career in the army.

Powell's fortunes would soon change once again. In the 1980 presidential election, the Republican party regained control of the White House, with former California governor Ronald Reagan soundly defeating Carter's bid for a second term in office. Reagan wasted little time in calling on an old friend, Caspar Weinberger, to head the Pentagon as defense secretary. Weinberger promptly tapped his deputy from the OMB, Frank Carlucci, for the post of deputy defense secretary. As they began to staff their department, both Carlucci and Weinberger remembered the promising young White House Fellow from their days at the OMB. Carlucci called Powell to the Pentagon, and when he invited the brigadier general to serve as his assistant once again, Powell accepted.

His first love, however, remained his role as soldier. Powell vastly preferred being a field commander to holding a bureaucratic position in the Pentagon. Yet the higher he rose on the military's ladder of success, the more removed he became from his desire to command troops. Since his last tour in Vietnam, he had spent only two years as a field commander: one in Korea and one with the 101st Airborne.

In the spring of 1981, Powell's wish to return to the field was granted; Weinberger appointed him assistant commander of the Fourth Infantry Division at Fort Carson, Colorado. Happy to be back with the troops, he spent the next two years at the post. In the spring of 1983 came a similiar assignment; this time, he was made the deputy commanding general of the Army Combined Arms Combat Development unit at Fort Leavenworth.

But Powell was not destined to remain in the field for very long. Events soon conspired to pull him away from his command and bring him back to the Pentagon. ◄❂►

Powell "is extraordinarily bright, articulate, and with excellent judgment," said Frank C. Carlucci, who became Powell's immediate boss at the State Department in 1972 and at the Pentagon in 1980. "Nobody could provide you with better guidance in this building or in the United States government."

6

WEATHERING
THE STORM

❧

A general discussion: General
Powell confers with General
Mikhail A. Moiseyev, the Soviet
Union's first minister of defense
and chief of the general staff,
aboard the USS Intrepid.
Meeting with foreign military
officials was one of the many
duties Powell performed during his
first decade with the Defense
Department.

IN THE SPRING of 1983, Defense Secretary
Caspar Weinberger began to search for a new senior
military assistant. The name he placed at the top of
the list of leading candidates was that of his former
colleague Colin Powell. Happily situated at Fort
Leavenworth, Powell had little desire to give up his
command. But when Weinberger contacted him, the
general knew enough to interview for the position.
His career might lose its momentum if he refused the
job outright.

Instead of declining the post, Powell told the
defense secretary that he preferred "being close to the
troops." His comment did little good. Weinberger
wanted Powell on his Pentagon staff, and so in June
1983 the general and his family reluctantly moved
back to Washington, D.C.

Powell may have displayed an initial lack of
enthusiasm for the position, but he certainly labored
hard at it. Emulating his father's work habits, he
arrived at the Pentagon every morning by 6:30 and
returned home after seven o'clock each evening. As

easygoing as he was tactful, he became indispensable to Weinberger. Powell screened staff members before they met with the defense secretary and reviewed memos and documents before they reached Weinberger to prevent unnecessary details from wasting the secretary's valuable time.

It did not take long for Powell to earn high marks for fairness from the department's employees. Not one to play favorites, he gave anyone who wished to speak with Weinberger a chance to do so. He clashed only with those who attempted to establish a private channel to the defense secretary.

Powell rarely expressed his own thoughts to Weinberger. He regarded his job as that of department coordinator; it was his duty to convey the staff members' views and ideas to the defense secretary. As a result, his Pentagon colleagues began to think of him, in the words of one associate, as "more of an expediter than a global thinker."

In effect, Powell functioned as Weinberger's chief of staff. According to Pentagon assistant secretary Michael Pillsbury, Powell "was the real secretary of defense. All paper, in or out, went through Colin. All meetings of substance Colin had to attend, or there was no meeting." An admiring Weinberger leaned heavily on his aide. He later remarked that Powell "knows what he's talking about and he always knows all of the buttons to push."

It did not take long for the Weinberger-Powell team to become the talk of the Pentagon. Wherever Weinberger went, Powell accompanied him. During Powell's tenure as senior military assistant, he traveled with Weinberger to more than 35 countries. Before long, Powell was awarded a second general's star and was elevated to the rank of major general.

Powell's performance as senior military assistant gained him not only Weinberger's confidence but also that of the Joint Chiefs of Staff. As a result, he was asked to play a major role in helping the Reagan administraion carry out a more aggressive approach to foreign policy.

The first time Powell took part in a major military action as a Pentagon official was when the United States invaded Grenada on October 25, 1983. Earlier in the month, revolutionaries on the tiny Caribbean island had put Maurice Bishop, the prime minister, under house arrest. This political coup threatened to strengthen the ties between Grenada's new Marxist government and both Cuba and the Soviet Union.

According to the Reagan administration, Grenada's association with the two Communist nations jeopardized American interests in the region. Moreover, its internal turmoil threatened American students who lived there. When the Organization of Eastern Caribbean States appealed to the United States to help restore order and democracy on Grenada, the president acted swiftly, sending 1,900 marines along with several hundred Caribbean troops to the island to overthrow the newly installed government.

Weinberger assigned Powell the task of convincing White House officials to allow the armed forces to carry out the invasion, code-named Urgent Fury, as the Defense Department saw fit. It also became Powell's responsibility to brief the White House about the course of the invasion. All told, the entire operation took less than a week to complete and was, according to government officials, an unqualified success.

Less successful was a scheme devised by Robert McFarlane, Reagan's national security adviser, to sell antitank and antiaircraft missiles to Iran. As head of the National Security Council staff, McFarlane was responsible for overseeing the operation of the staff

Powell served as senior military adviser to Secretary of Defense Caspar W. Weinberger from 1983 to 1986. Powell, Weinberger said, "is one of the very best persons I have ever worked with in any of the positions I've had. He has excelled in everything he has touched, and he always will. I don't think you can find anyone who has anything bad to say about Colin Powell, which is an extraordinary thing when you've been around Washington as long as he has—in highly sensitive and vital assignments."

as well as the workings of the NSC system. But he was hoping to accomplish far more than that.

The NSC had been formed in 1947 to serve as a forum for advising the president on matters relating to the nation's security. Attending the NSC meetings in addition to the president are the vice-president, the state and defense secretaries, the chairman of the JCS, the director of the Central Intelligence Agency (CIA), and the so-called NSC adviser, whose actual title is assistant to the president for national security affairs. The civilian and military officials who make up the NSC advisory staff contribute to the proceedings by monitoring the world situation, coordinating research involving various government agencies, and providing information and recommendations to the council.

The NSC staff was established in part to act as a watchdog, curbing the competition between the State and Defense departments as they shaped foreign policy. Over the years, however, NSC advisers managed to broaden their influence in American affairs by turning their agency into an independent policy-making body. Henry Kissinger, for one, virtually controlled the nation's foreign policy when he served as NSC adviser during the Nixon administration.

McFarlane, too, attempted to exercise his power, but he did it in a way that threatened to bring down the entire Reagan administration. The first hint that he had exceeded his authority came in the summer of 1985, as Powell was entering his third year as senior military assistant. Powell received an apparently routine request from the NSC. It wanted information on the price and availability of sophisticated TOW wire-guided antitank missiles for sale abroad.

Powell delivered the information, considering his action, as he later explained to the *Washington Post*, "a routine service that I would provide to any department." He did not know that McFarlane was planning to sell the TOW missiles to win the release of American hostages held in Lebanon by Iranian-backed Islamic extremists.

McFarlane's scheme violated both the president's policy of not aiding Iran during its ongoing war with neighboring Iraq and his publicly stated promise not to make bargains with terrorist groups. Despite these strong words, Reagan's loose management style allowed the NSC staff to sell war matériel to Iran without his approval or any other form of official supervision. On August 20, 1985, the NSC staff put the plan into operation, making a small arms delivery to Israel, America's chief ally in the Middle East. Acting as go-between, the Israelis bought the missiles from the United States and then shipped them to Iran. Approaching the deal in this circuitous way allowed McFarlane to maintain he was not doing anything illegal.

After the NSC staff inquired about the TOW missiles, it approached Powell for information about HAWK antiaircraft missiles. Meanwhile, McFarlane arranged to ship more TOW missiles to Iran. A second delivery was made on September 14.

Both Powell and Weinberger, along with Secretary of State George Shultz, opposed the arms deal as soon as they uncovered what the NSC staff was up to. But they were unable to stop it. In January 1986, one month after McFarlane resigned as national security adviser, the new head of the NSC staff, Rear Admiral John Poindexter, persuaded Reagan to authorize direct arms shipments to Iran in the hope of winning the hostages' release. Now that the deal had the president's approval, Weinberger chose Powell to carry out the transfer of weapons from Pentagon stockpiles to the CIA, which arranged to ship them to Iran.

Despite the presidential order to go ahead with the sale, the attempt to exchange arms for hostages still troubled Powell. He wrote a memo to Poindexter, reminding him of the legal requirement to notify Congress of any arms transfers, such as those that were now taking place. Poindexter, well aware of the outcry that would result if Congress found out about the arms sales and of the potential political damage to the president if the scheme was uncovered, ignored Powell's memo.

Powell chafed to get away from Washington, D.C., and return to a field command. In June 1986, Weinberger let him go. Powell was appointed to command the U.S. Army V Corps stationed in

Lieutenant Colonel Oliver L. North is sworn in at a 1987 investigation into the Iran-contra affair. Powell was among the few people implicated in the wide-ranging scandal to be found innocent of any wrongdoing.

Frankfurt, West Germany. This assignment put him directly in charge of 72,000 active-duty combat troops. At the same time, Reagan authorized Powell's promotion to lieutenant general, the army's third-highest rank, superseded only by full general and general of the army. With a prestigious field command and three stars sewn on his shoulder, Powell said that he was "probably the happiest general in the world."

A few months later, the storm broke. On November 13, the president appeared on television to confirm reports that the United States had secretly sold arms to Iran, and a national uproar ensued. The situation grew worse when Attorney General Edwin Meese revealed that the NSC staff had diverted part of the $48 million Iran had paid for the arms, using the funds to supply military aid to the contra rebels fighting Nicaragua's Sandinista government.

This second scheme, run by NSC staff member U.S. Marine Corps lieutenant colonel Oliver L. North, directly violated a 1984 law passed by Congress that prohibited all military aid, direct or indirect, to the contras. Poindexter had supported North's illegal operation and had deliberately concealed it from the president. Reagan appointed a review board headed by former senator John Tower to investigate the scandal.

The Tower Commission found among the documents concerning NSC operations a note handwritten by North. The memo listed the people in the government who knew about the secret arms deals with Iran. Third on the list of 16 people, after Shultz and Weinberger, stood the name of Colin Powell.

The general testified privately in front of congressional committees about his role in the scandal, which became popularly known as the Iran-contra affair. He testified alone, in private sessions, because

Congress felt it inappropriate to question him publicly alongside Pentagon officials of lower rank.

The investigators found no evidence of any
wrongdoing on Powell's part. He had acted as a staff
member rather than as a policymaker and had properly followed orders from his superiors in coordinating
arms transfers to the CIA. The discovery of his memo
to Poindexter, reminding the national security adviser of his responsibility to notify Congress of the
arms sales, won Powell respect and approval on
Capitol Hill. He emerged from the Iran-contra scandal as one of the few participants to survive with an
unblemished reputation. ◄◊►

7

"MR. PRESIDENT, I'M A SOLDIER"

W HEN COLIN POWELL was told he was being appointed commander of the Army V Corps, he anticipated a long tour of duty in West Germany. He had seen enough of Washington, D.C.'s political jungle to realize all over again that he preferred being stationed with the troops. He also hoped his new assignment would lead to a promotion as the U.S. Army's chief of staff. Therefore, when Frank Carlucci called him six months into his command with an offer of a new White House position, Powell instantly responded, "No way."

Carlucci had recently accepted a new job, too. The Iran-contra affair had forced John Poindexter to resign as national security adviser, and in a bid to restore the National Security Council's tarnished image, President Ronald Reagan had appointed the universally respected Carlucci as Poindexter's replacement. Carlucci saw at once that the scandal had left the credibility of the 190-member NSC staff on the brink of collapse, and he desperately needed someone with Powell's diplomatic and leadership skills to help rebuild the shattered organization. That was why he had telephoned Powell in Frankfurt: to ask his former assistant to become deputy national security adviser.

Powell gives President Ronald Reagan his daily 30-minute briefing on national security. "I'm principally a broker," Powell said of being deputy national security adviser and national security adviser, posts he held from January 1987 to January 1989. "I have strong views on things, but my job is to make sure the president gets the best information available to make an informed decision."

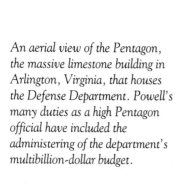
An aerial view of the Pentagon, the massive limestone building in Arlington, Virginia, that houses the Defense Department. Powell's many duties as a high Pentagon official have included the administering of the department's multibillion-dollar budget.

Powell's refusal did not discourage Carlucci. He called twice more in an effort to get Powell to change his mind. On the third try, Carlucci sounded so desperate that a wavering Powell phoned him back and pleaded his involvement in the Iran-contra affair as a reason for rejecting the post. "Frank," he said, "you should know I've been questioned about Iran-contra because of those TOW missiles and may be asked to testify. That could be a problem."

"Colin, I've talked to everybody," Carlucci responded. "You're clean. I wouldn't ask you to give up this command if I didn't need you. The commander in chief needs you."

"If he really wants me," Powell said reluctantly, "then I have to do it."

The next evening, Powell's phone rang again. When he picked up the receiver, he heard the president's voice on the line. Reagan attempted to add his own influence to Carlucci's pleas. "I know you've been looking forward to this command," the president told Powell, "but we need you here." It was unthinkable to Powell to turn down a request from one's commander in chief. "Mr. President, I'm a soldier," he replied, "and if I can help, I'll come."

Powell rejoined Carlucci in Washington, D.C., at the beginning of 1987. Together the two men began the task of restoring life to the NSC. Powell took over the job of reorganizing the staff to comply with recommendations made by the Tower Commission. Poindexter had kept all NSC departments separate from each other, which had allowed Oliver North to run his illegal contra operation without control or comment from any other part of the NSC. Powell introduced a clear chain of command while at the same time encouraging discussion among the NSC staff and related government agencies on most policy items.

"Like Frank," Powell said, "I am a great believer that the interagency process works best when everybody has a chance to say his piece and get his positions out on the table. . . . When we forward the final decision package to the president or present it to him orally, everybody who played knows he has been properly represented and had his day in court." Under Carlucci and Powell's leadership, the NSC staff revived quickly and began to assume its proper place in the government.

Carlucci occasionally broke with NSC tradition by letting his deputy give the president his daily 30-minute briefing on national security. Carlucci hoped to give Powell a chance to develop a personal relationship with the chief executive, and he was not disappointed; Reagan instantly took a liking to the general. The president appreciated that Powell treated him courteously but without the overzealousness that many senior military officers displayed in his presence. The two men also shared a common bond: Each had been a youthful underachiever who had nonetheless managed to become a success.

For his part, Powell failed to show any resentment toward Reagan over the president's opposition to several pieces of civil rights legislation aimed at advancing blacks' rights. The general contented himself with working slowly to improve the president's sensitivity to the problems of black America.

Shortly after Powell took over as Carlucci's deputy, a tragic accident almost robbed him and Alma of their only son. Michael had followed his father into the army and at the age of 24 had become a first lieutenant. He was stationed in West Germany when his jeep overturned, breaking the young officer's pelvis in six places. Four days after the accident, Michael arrived at Walter Reed Army Hospital in Washington, D.C., for surgery.

A stunned Powell sat by his son's bed, fearful that Michael might not survive and that if he did, he might have to spend the rest of his life in a wheelchair. "You'll make it!" the general repeatedly said to his son, practically willing him to live. "You want to make it, so you will make it!"

Michael survived the surgery but remained in the hospital for a year. Then he returned to his parents' home in Fort Meyer, Virginia, to convalesce. Continual therapy eventually enabled him to walk again. When he was finally fit enough to go back to work, he left the army and joined the Defense Department.

On November 5, 1987, while Michael was still in the hospital, a changing of the guard in the Reagan administration placed Colin Powell in a leading role on the national stage for the first time. This newly won position came Powell's way when Caspar Weinberger approached Howard Baker, Reagan's chief of

National Security Adviser Powell discusses a proposal for a United States–Soviet Union medium-range missile treaty with (from left to right) White House Chief of Staff Howard Baker, Senator Robert Dole, and Senator Alan Simpson. This meeting was held as part of the preparations for a May 1988 summit conference between President Ronald Reagan and Soviet Union leader Mikhail S. Gorbachev.

staff, and said he wanted to resign as defense secretary. Baker promptly escorted Weinberger to the Oval Office to talk over the situation with the president.

Reagan accepted Weinberger's resignation after the latter assured him the main reason why he wished to leave the government was his wife's poor health. The president then began to discuss with Weinberger and Baker who should become the next defense secretary. All three men agreed on Carlucci. There was one last matter to settle: Who should succeed Carlucci as national security adviser? Powell's name was suggested. "I think that's a great idea," Reagan responded. "Nobody else was considered," Baker later said of the meeting.

Indeed, Powell's reputation for integrity and his hand in rebuilding the NSC staff made him a doubly good choice. Moreover, his lack of a personal political agenda recommended him as an administrator who could continue to restore the NSC to its proper role as a watchdog over the State and Defense departments.

Only one issue stood a chance of preventing Powell's appointment. After uncovering Rear Admiral John Poindexter's role in the Iran-contra affair, the Tower Commission had strongly recommended that no military officer ever again be appointed national security adviser. Powell himself agreed with the commission's recommendation. In October 1987, just one month prior to Weinberger's resignation, Powell had told the *New York Times* that in his opinion only civilians should fill this sensitive post.

Yet Powell was by now so popular in government circles that his nomination to the post of national security adviser met with few objections. He continued to state that he supported the idea of a civilian serving as national security adviser. But Powell also said publicly that "the transcendent principle is that a President should have who he wants."

In late December 1987, Powell became Reagan's sixth national security adviser. The 10 months he had spent as Carlucci's deputy enabled the 50-year-old general to adapt smoothly to the national security adviser's daily routine. At 6:30 each morning, he arrived at his corner office on the first floor of the White House's west wing. For 30 minutes, he studied intelligence reports on military and political activities around the world. At 7:00 A.M., Carlucci and Secretary of State George Shultz joined him for a conference. After two more hours of private conversations and phone calls, Powell seated himself on a sofa across from Reagan and gave the chief executive his daily national security briefing.

"It was a heck of a homework quiz," Powell later said of these presidential briefings. "I would give him warning of what was coming our way, or sometimes just philosophize: for example, what was happening

General Powell and First Captain Cadet Kristin Baker, the U.S. Military Academy's first female brigade commander, meet the press at West Point. In recent years, Powell has made himself accessible to the public so as to encourage others to rise as high as they can. "If you check my stats around here," he told Ebony magazine, "you'll find I've been to elementary schools, junior high schools, high schools trying to get the message out every way I can."

in the Soviet Union or how Congress was reacting to a particular issue. It was a challenge, but it becomes a natural one because you're doing it every day."

The president and the soldier maintained the cordial relationship they had established during Powell's tenure as Carlucci's deputy. As was his style, Powell did not press his views on Reagan but tried to influence him with carefully reasoned arguments. The general's tact and persuasiveness, for example, played a large part in convincing the president to back away from his cherished policy of sending the contras military aid in their fight against the Sandinista government of Nicaragua. Although Powell personally supported the rebels' goals, his political instincts told him an attempt to send more military aid to the contras would not survive the public's outrage over the Iran-contra affair. Instead he helped persuade Reagan to push for a face-saving compromise that would allow shipments of food and medicine to the rebels but ban all transfers of arms.

In fulfilling his role as national security adviser, Powell tried to avoid appearing overly sympathetic to the military point of view. He also worked long and hard at locating a middle ground in disputes between the State and Defense departments over foreign policy. Cabinet politics in the waning days of the Reagan administration often made this task difficult. No longer opposed by the strong and crusty Caspar Weinberger, George Shultz tried to assume control of the administration's foreign policy. As a result, Powell was often forced to back Carlucci to keep the balance of power between the State and Defense departments intact.

Powell usually handled these disputes with the utmost diplomacy. When Shultz suggested various ways to remove Panamanian dictator Manuel Antonio Noriega from power, such as kidnapping him or setting up a rival government in exile, Powell did not immediately tell the secretary of state that he opposed the plan. Instead he checked with other NSC members to see how they felt about Shultz's proposal. Discovering that they opposed it as well, Powell convened a fully staffed NSC meeting. Arranging for the matter to be discussed in an open forum let Shultz see for himself that it was not the general alone who disapproved of the plan.

There was only one aspect of his job that Powell did not appear to relish: the constant media exposure. Now that he was the administration's national security spokesman, every word he uttered in public seemed to take on special significance. His newfound visibility prompted Powell to remark to an interviewer, "You'd better have a hell of a lot of information [as a White House official]. You cannot be wrong. If you're wrong, you're a headline."

Powell also complained about the weekly ritual of talking to reporters. "Why do I have to talk to these people every week?" he asked White House press spokesman Marlin Fitzwater shortly after taking over as national security adviser. "All they ever want to know is who did what to whom. They never ask about substance."

Powell may have viewed the media as a necessary evil, but reporters liked the general. He had got off on the right foot, winning their respect during his first month as national security adviser. While accompanying the president to a lavish New Year's Eve celebration in Palm Springs, California, he had dropped in on a party for the Reagan press corps. A television producer, having heard that the general might show up, had arranged a surprise or two to test Powell's mettle.

The producer had ordered a pair of cakes to be baked for the party, both of which were meant to recall the sins of past national security advisers. One of the desserts was molded to look like a key, to serve

Side boys salute General Powell as he arrives for a change-of-command ceremony on the USS John F. Kennedy. Powell was promoted to the rank of four-star general in 1989.

as a reminder of the time Robert McFarlane had brought a key-shaped cake (to symbolize the unlocking of doors) to a secret meeting in Iran during the arms-for-hostages deal. The other cake, in the shape of a Bible, was baked in honor of a trip to Iran that John Poindexter's associate Oliver North had made in support of the deal; the lieutenant colonel had brought his Iranian contacts a Bible signed by the president.

Powell did not lose his composure for an instant when he spotted the cakes. Instead he shared in the joke—to the point of posing with them for photographs. "That's Colin Powell," said one of the reporters on hand. "He's a General but a damn nice guy."

Regardless of how much Powell disliked dealing with the media, he became very good at it. His role in coordinating the efforts of policymakers and technical advisers during the December 1987 summit conference between Reagan and Soviet Union leader Mikhail S. Gorbachev resulted in his making frequent appearances on television news broadcasts. Powell developed a calm, cool, and self-possessed persona for the screen. The only time he lost his composure in front of the cameras occurred when a reporter for the "Nightwatch" news program asked him a personal question about his parents. Powell could not speak for a moment. Finally, he said in a voice full of emotion, "Well, Mom, Pop, you brought us up right. All of us. I hope you're happy. I hope you're proud of what we do."

The media naturally focused on Powell's race, but he felt strongly that it should not influence people's judgment of him. "What my color is is someone else's problem, not mine," he told a television interviewer. "People will say, 'You're a terrific Black general.' I'm trying to be the best general I can be." Nonetheless, he recognized that by working hard and earning respect for his abilities, he was helping to open doors to other blacks.

Powell tried to be more than just a role model. He made himself accessible to interviewers representing black publications, spoke out against racism at public appearances, and lent his support to the civil rights movement as best he could from the Reagan White House. "I am . . . mindful that the struggle [against racism] is not over," he said at a January 1988 meeting of a black political studies organization, ". . . until every American is able to find his or her own place in our society, limited by his or her own ability and his or her own dream."

An incident that occurred shortly after Powell took over as national security adviser demonstrated the importance he attached to supporting black rights. A blizzard broke out on the day he was scheduled to speak at a luncheon given by one of Washington, D.C.'s oldest black patriotic organizations, the James Reese Europe American Legion Post. When his secretary offered to cancel the appointment because of the foul weather, Powell simply responded, "No, I have to go." He then spent 2 hours driving through the snow to give a half-hour speech to 12 people on the contributions of blacks to the American military.

Although Powell supported the civil rights movement, many black leaders felt he was betraying his race by serving a president whom they viewed as hostile to their cause. During a speech Powell gave in January 1988 at the Joint Center for Political Studies, several black officials walked out of the room after he began to speak in favor of the administration's policy to continue business ties with South Africa, a nation that endorsed racial segregation. Powell "will not attain hero status from the masses of black people," said civil rights leader and politician Jesse L. Jackson, "because Reagan has been so indifferent . . . to blacks."

Powell disagreed with Jackson. "Surprisingly, most black American groups I talk to are proud of the fact that I have this job," he told the press. "The fact that I have this job is a credit to the President. . . . He knew me and he gave it to me." Despite their differences, Jackson and Powell have developed a warm friendship, each admiring what the other has accomplished.

Indeed, Powell has succeeded in leaving almost no political enemies in his wake. Even his occasional opponent George Shultz has honored him. In September 1988, the secretary of state bestowed on Powell the Secretary's Award, given out annually for "distinguished contributions to the development, management, or implementation" of U.S. foreign policy. Shultz cited Powell for his role in coordinating Reagan's two summit meetings with Gorbachev.

Powell's widespread popularity prompted many political observers to call on George Bush, who was on course to succeed Reagan in the White House, to make Powell his running mate during the 1988 presidential election. Other people had their own ideas about where Powell's career was headed. NSC insiders regarded him as a strong candidate for U.S. Army chief of staff, a position that was to open up in early 1990. Frank Carlucci, who said that Powell had done a better job running the NSC staff than he had, speculated that the general might even become chairman of the Joint Chiefs of Staff.

As the end of Reagan's second term in office drew near, not even Powell could predict what his own future might hold. Rumors began to spread that he would be asked to stay on as national security adviser if Bush won the 1988 presidential election, but Powell brushed them aside and waited until all the votes were in. Bush won the election handily; a short time later, he called in Powell and delivered the news. "I think I ought to have my own national security adviser," said the president-elect.

When word began to spread that Powell would be leaving his White House post, U.S. Army chief of staff General Carl Vuono phoned him with an offer. "If you want to come home to the army, we have a job for you," Vuono said. A New York City booking agent approached Powell as well, telling him he could make far more money on the lecture circuit than he could in the army. The speech agent offered Powell a contract worth more than $100,000.

The general was so overwhelmed by his choices that he sat down with a pen and a sheet of paper and made two columns. He labeled one of them "Reasons to stay in the army" and the other "Reasons to leave the army." He easily found a dozen items to put in the first column; he wrote only one word under the second heading: *Money*. Powell decided to follow his heart and return to active duty in the army.

Before Reagan left office, the president followed through on Vuono's offer and promoted Powell to the rank of four-star general. He also named Powell commander in chief of the U.S. Forces Command at Fort McPherson in Atlanta, Georgia. With this appointment, the former ROTC graduate found himself in charge of all the army's troops in the continental United States. The men and women under his authority included 250,000 active-duty troops and 300,000 reserves. If, as happens in a time of crisis, the National Guard was to be activated, Powell would control more than 1 million soldiers, or almost two-thirds of the army's worldwide combat strength. ❧

8

THE BEST MAN FOR
THE JOB

❧

Powell listens to a military briefing at Panamanian dictator Manuel Noriega's headquarters on January 5, 1990. Sending U.S. troops into Panama to take Noriega's compound was one of the military actions that Powell has overseen as JCS chairman.

IN EARLY 1989, as Colin Powell assumed his post as commander in chief of the U.S. Forces Command, George Bush took over the reins of the federal government. Powell felt distant from the incoming regime, separated by more than the miles between Washington, D.C., and Atlanta. Personal alliances were very important to the new president, and Powell could not claim any close bonds of friendship to Bush's inner circle—certainly not in the way that his association with Frank Carlucci and Caspar Weinberger had tied him to Ronald Reagan.

What's more, the 1988 presidential campaign had left the general feeling uneasy about Bush. His campaign had tried to stir up racial fears by running a television commercial about Willie Horton, a convicted black rapist who had been furloughed from prison under a Massachusetts law supported by Governor Michael S. Dukakis, the Democratic candidate in the race. While on leave, Horton had raped a white woman—a crime that the commercial blamed on Dukakis, implying that rampaging blacks would threaten the nation if the governor were elected president. This smear tactic deeply disturbed Powell and added to his misgivings about the new administration. Consequently, when the president offered to make him director of the CIA, Powell turned Bush down.

There appeared to be only one government position that would entice the general into returning to Washington, D.C. In August 1989, it came his way. The new secretary of defense, Dick Cheney, a member of the House Intelligence Committee during Powell's term as national security adviser, phoned him with an offer to become chairman of the JCS. "I have recommended that the president appoint you," said Cheney, who held Powell in very high regard. "He has accepted my recommendation."

After his conversation with Cheney, Powell called his wife. "Alma," he said, "we're moving again. The president's making me chairman of the Joint Chiefs."

The choice of Powell to replace the retiring JCS chairman, William Crowe, Jr., met with widespread praise. But approval of Powell's appointment was not unanimous. A number of high-ranking military officers resented the fact that the president had bypassed dozens of candidates with more seniority in favor of a general who had received his fourth star just a few months earlier and had spent more time holding government jobs than commanding combat troops.

Powell, these officers grumbled, had climbed to the chairmanship on his political connections rather than on his military expertise. "In his last 20 years in the service, he served 5 years with the operational units and the other 15 years in Washington," retired rear admiral Eugene Carroll told the *Congressional Quarterly*. As a result, many younger officers would interpret Powell's success as a cue to "come to Washington; serve your political mentors; make

friends where it counts . . . and avoid those trips to the troops."

Powell's lack of long-term command experience had also caused Bush and Cheney some concern. Cheney had originally favored appointing Crowe's deputy as chairman, which would have permitted Powell to spend the next two years getting more seasoning as a commander before moving into the JCS chairmanship when the position reopened in 1989. After considering their options more closely, both Bush and Cheney decided that Powell was already the best man for the job.

Powell officially became the JCS chairman on October 3, 1989. According to a government observer writing about the general at one of his first JCS meetings, "If a stranger had come into the room and been told that one person there was new to his job, he would never guess it was Powell. The new

Defense Secretary Dick Cheney (left) confers with Powell at a Senate Armed Services Committee hearing. The top two officials in the Defense Department, Cheney and Powell have worked closely together since the latter became JCS chairman on October 3, 1989.

Chairman was utterly confident. He absolutely filled the room. There was a quality about him that announced, 'Hi, get the hell out of the way, I'm Chairman.'"

World events quickly put Powell to the test. Within his first few months in office, the American military had to deal with small crises in Panama, the Philippines, and El Salvador. The quick succession of these events prompted Powell to comment afterward, "I've had several cold showers. From time to time, when you least expect it, when everyone thinks the world is quiet, someone pulls on Superman's cape."

In the first emergency, revolutionaries eager to overthrow Panamanian dictator Manuel Noriega sought American assistance; certain that an attempted coup was destined to fail, Powell recommended against aiding the rebels. The second international crisis involved another military coup, this one in the Philippines, where the United States had an important air base and naval station; the JCS chairman advocated the use of American warplanes to put down the rebellion. Powell's third "cold shower" occurred when a civil war in El Salvador placed some Green Berets, part of the U.S. Army's special-operations force, in grave danger; Powell called for additional troops to go into San Salvador to rescue the soldiers.

In late 1989, Powell met with Bush to discuss an even more sensitive assignment. The president, outraged by the international drug-smuggling activities encouraged by Noriega, wanted the Panamanian dictator physically removed from power. Powell preferred to negotiate a deal with Noriega: The United States would drop all drug-smuggling charges against him if he would relinquish control of the government.

Powell changed his mind, however, when Noriega's soldiers killed a U.S. marine in Panama. The JCS chairman spent the better part of the next two months with General Maxwell R. Thurman of the Southern Command, devising a plan for 26,000 U.S. troops to invade Panama and hunt down Noriega. Their plan became known as Operation Just Cause.

The American invasion commenced on December 20. "We will chase him," Powell said of Noriega as Operation Just Cause unfolded, "and we will find him." As promised, the operation proved swift and successful. Unprepared for such a massive, lightning-like strike, Noriega was cornered by U.S. military forces and brought to Florida to face drug-trafficking charges.

Throughout Operation Just Cause, Powell held frequent press briefings to let the American public know that its troops were in total command of the operation. Ever since the Vietnam War, the nation's military leaders had shied away from sending soldiers into combat for fear of a public outcry over the resulting casualties. Powell's experiences in Vietnam had convinced him that a halfhearted commitment of troops, no matter how sophisticated their weaponry, achieved little against a determined enemy. Such an approach led only to a prolonged conflict, with plenty of casualties and little public support.

In situations that called for military force, Powell preferred to make the initial blow strong enough to guarantee a quick, clean success. "Strike suddenly, decisively, and in sufficient force to resolve the matter" was his opinion. "Do it quickly; and . . . do it with a minimum loss of life."

Despite this philosophy, Powell was never especially eager to use force. He had, in fact, taped to his Pentagon desk a quotation from the ancient Greek historian Thucydides: "Of all manifestations of power, restraint impresses men most." Powell had seen the horrors of battle in Vietnam and understood there was no such thing as a risk-free operation or a clean bombing attack. What's more, he knew that another inconclusive war, like the one in Vietnam, would

Powell addresses crew members aboard the battleship USS Wisconsin, stationed in the Persian Gulf as part of Operation Desert Shield, in September 1990, one month after Iraqi troops invaded Kuwait. To prepare for the deployment of American forces in the Middle East, Powell intensively studied the history of the region. "I always like to have a context for what I do," he said, "so I know I'm in the right stadium and I'm playing the right game. Then I can go on the field and play it. History helps put me in that context."

seriously jeopardize the standing of the American military both at home and abroad.

Yet by early 1991, Powell would find himself in charge of the largest U.S. military action since Vietnam.

On August 2, 1990, the Bush administration was stunned by reports that 80,000 Iraqi troops commanded by President Saddam Hussein had just invaded neighboring Kuwait. Iraq's military action gave Hussein control of Kuwait's vast oil fields and put his army in position to strike further southward, into oil-rich Saudi Arabia. The fear that Iraq, which boasted the Middle East's largest and best-equipped army, would soon gain control of most of the world's oil supply forced oil prices to rise sharply and sent shock waves through almost every nation's economy.

Bush responded to the invasion with a firm warning. Hussein's action "will not stand," he promised the American public. "This will not stand."

Privately, Powell was dismayed to hear Bush promising to liberate Kuwait without first consulting his military leadership. Moreover, the general favored a strategy of containing Hussein's ambitions with economic sanctions, not with the use of force. In public, however, Powell backed his president and advised him that a token show of strength would not intimidate Hussein into withdrawing from Kuwait. "You can't put a ship in the [Persian] Gulf and lob shells and do anything," Powell said. If the president really wanted to turn back the Iraqi army and at the same time reaffirm America's role as a preeminent world power, he should act quickly and send as many troops to the Persian Gulf as possible.

At Bush's behest, Powell drew up the plans for what became known as Operation Desert Shield, the largest deployment of American forces since the Vietnam War. Within days after Bush approved of the plan, U.S. troops began to arrive in the Saudi Arabian desert, where they were joined by a coalition of United Nations (UN) forces. By November, 180,000 U.S. soldiers were stationed near the Saudi border, keeping a watch on Hussein's army across the desert in Iraq and Kuwait.

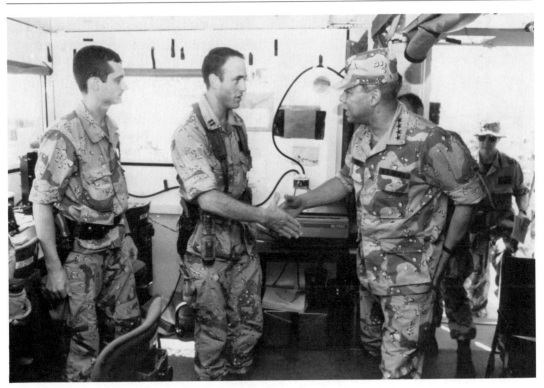

The Bush administration's rapid deployment of troops did not go uncriticized in the States. Many people said they did not want to see American lives lost in what they regarded as a purely foreign dispute. Undeterred, Powell defended the use of U.S. troops to help settle an international affair. "I certainly agree that we should not go around saying that we are the world's policeman," he said, "but guess who gets called when suddenly someone needs a cop."

Donning the mantle of international peacekeeper did not seem to go far enough, according to the president and his defense secretary. Neither the defensive position of the coalition-led forces nor the economic sanctions that the UN had imposed on Iraq were convincing Hussein to withdraw. As a result, Bush and Cheney told Powell on November 8 to double the American presence in the Persian Gulf. The added troop strength would not only improve

Powell greets U.S. airmen while visiting military facilities in the Saudi Arabian desert during the Persian Gulf war. Said one of his associates, "If there was ever anybody who could communicate with the private fixing a broken tank tread and in the next second talk with the president, it's Colin Powell."

Saudi Arabia's defenses but also give the allied forces enough offensive capabilities to confront Iraq.

Powell did not support the idea of launching a desert offensive in the Middle East. Fearing that, as in the Vietnam War, thousands of American soldiers would die needlessly and that such an outcome would erode public support for the military, he preferred to continue pressuring Iraq with economic sanctions. But when Powell told his opinion to the president, Bush responded, "I don't think there's time politically for that strategy."

Accordingly, Powell set about turning the president's wishes into reality. He began to orchestrate a massive build up of troops and tanks, ships and aircraft, in the Middle East. As he told the Senate Armed Services Committee, "My job is to make sure that if it is necessary to go to war, we go to war to win." If diplomacy could not resolve the crisis, Iraq would receive the full weight of allied military might in swift and crushing blows.

At a press conference, Powell outlined in simple terms the strategy for defeating the Iraqi army. "First we're going to cut it off," he said, "and then we're going to kill it." All the while, he hoped that the two months it would take to transform Operation Desert Shield into Operation Desert Storm, an attack force large enough to defeat Iraq's 1 million-man army, was enough time for the crisis to be resolved peacefully.

In early December, another alarm for war sounded: The UN Security Council authorized "all necessary means" to expel Hussein from Kuwait if he did not withdraw his troops by January 15, 1991. "Should military action be required," Bush told the American public, "this will not be another Vietnam. This will not be a protracted, drawn-out war."

To make sure the allied victory would be rapid, Powell met separately with White House officials and the nation's military leaders, acting as a liaison

A longtime acquaintance of Powell's, General H. Norman Schwarzkopf was the chief architect of Operation Desert Storm, the 1991 campaign to liberate Kuwait from occupying Iraqi troops. Powell served as Schwarzkopf's link to the president and Congress during the Persian Gulf war and was responsible for convincing the government to support what proved to be a very successful military plan.

between the two. He let the strategists under his command—particularly the head of U.S. Central Command in Saudi Arabia, General H. Norman Schwarzkopf—work out the details of the military operation; Powell took it upon himself to convince the president and Congress of the resulting plan's merit. He also coordinated the United States' war strategies with those of its allies. Making stops throughout Europe and the Middle East, he established a unified command-and-control system for the 18 nations preparing to engage in battle with Iraq.

On January 15, the UN deadline passed without Hussein withdrawing his forces from Kuwait. Less than 24 hours later, multinational forces unleashed a massive air assault on the Iraqis. It was the largest air strike in history. Allied forces flew more than 1,000 missions in the first 14 hours of combat, more than

President George Bush (fourth from right) holds a national security briefing in the White House's Oval Office on February 25, 1991, the day after allied forces launched a ground offensive in the Persian Gulf war.
Attending the meeting are (from left to right) Powell, Chief of Staff John Sununu, Defense Secretary Dick Cheney, Vice-president Dan Quayle, Secretary of State James A. Baker III, and National Security Adviser Brent Scowcroft and his deputy Robert Gates.

double the number of sorties flown by U.S. pilots during the heaviest period of fighting in Vietnam.

By February 23, continued allied air strikes had paralyzed Iraq's military command-and-communications systems and had saddled the Iraqi army with tremendous losses. At that point, allied ground troops went on the offensive. One hundred hours later, the Iraqi president, with his army in shambles and virtually cut off from all means of retreat, agreed to withdraw from Kuwait and meet every other UN demand.

The speedy, complete, and relatively bloodless victory for the allies—less than 200 Americans were killed in the Persian Gulf war—turned Powell, Schwarzkopf, and the rest of the U.S. military into national heroes. Congressmen proposed to promote the two men to the rank of General of the Army, which would make them the first generals to wear five stars since Omar N. Bradley was accorded that honor in 1950. In addition, both officers reminded people of an equally popular military leader, general-turned-statesman Dwight D. Eisenhower, and they began to hear their names mentioned as potential political candidates.

Powell did not like the sudden barrage of attention that surrounded him in the months following the end of the Persian Gulf war. He commented despairingly to a colleague about the growing political speculation, "I can't tell you how much I hate this. I don't control my life anymore."

For a while, Powell tried to avoid publicity as much as possible, to the point of asking *U.S. News and World Report* to substitute a planned cover story on him with one on Schwarzkopf. (The magazine refused his request.) In the relatively few free moments he had left to himself, Powell pursued a favorite hobby—repairing broken-down Volvos—and spent time with his wife and three children: Michael, 28, a student at Georgetown University's law school; Linda, 26, a television actress and employed in New York at a major corporation; and Annemarie, 20, a junior at the College of William and Mary.

To questions about his political future, Powell gave a standard response: "I have no interest in politics at the moment." Yet the constant rumors that he would replace Vice-president Dan Quayle on Bush's 1992 reelection ticket deeply bothered Powell. In mid-March 1991, the JCS chairman finally felt compelled to telephone the vice-president and state outright that he had no desire to become the president's running mate in the next election. Powell's actions subsequently bore him out. That May, he accepted Bush's invitation to serve two more years as JCS chairman, which precludes him from seeking any other employment until his second term as chairman ends in 1993.

Powell and his wife, Alma, along with Defense Secretary Dick Cheney (fourth from left), greet returning prisoners of war, including U.S. Navy lieutenant Jeffrey Zaun (third from left), at Maryland's Andrews Air Force Base on March 10, 1991. Powell's resolute, commanding image appeared often in the media during the Persian Gulf war and helped boost his standing with the American public.

In the meantime, formidable challenges await Chairman Powell. The Bush administration, facing continual pressure to lower the massive federal debt, has been urged to cut the national defense budget. Powell has agreed that military spending should be decreased, especially in light of the end of the cold war and the Soviet Union's greatly reduced global ambitions. But he has also made it clear that the armed forces have to remain well funded if they are to respond effectively to regional crises such as the one in the Persian Gulf. "Peace through strength vanishes as a possibility," he told journalist Carl Rowan, "if there is no strength."

In the months following the Persian Gulf war, Powell went to work restructuring the U.S. military in response to a declining Pentagon budget. He teamed up with Cheney and other Defense Department officials in determining which domestic bases could be closed down or consolidated without causing serious disruptions to military operations. In addition, he contended with being a role model, which he regarded as one of the most important—and most gratifying—offshoots of his job. Reaching the top of the military, he said, has helped raise "the expectation level a little higher" for other blacks.

But not all blacks were supportive of Powell's high position. Shortly before the start of the Persian Gulf war, he withdrew as marshal of a parade honoring Martin Luther King, Jr., because associates of the slain civil rights leader felt that being a JCS chairman was not in keeping with King's commitment to nonviolence. Several months later, the audience at a Congressional Black Caucus meeting told Powell they were upset that a disproportionately large number of blacks had been asked to risk their life in the Persian Gulf war. (According to the Defense Department, blacks made up only 12 percent of American society but accounted for 25 percent of the forces in the Persian Gulf.)

In defense of the military, Powell echoed Bush's words: "To those who question the proportion of blacks in the armed services," the president said on February 25, "my answer is simple. The military of the United States is the greatest equal opportunity employer around."

Powell could have answered the critics just as easily by telling them about his trip to Fort Leavenworth less than a year earlier. In July 1990, he returned to the Kansas military base to break ground for a memorial to the Ninth and 10th Cavalry regiments, a project he had launched during his tenure as deputy commanding general. The monument was being built on the site of the former Buffalo Soldiers' barracks, and by digging into the soil, Powell had taken part in a ceremony to honor the black soldiers who had struggled long and hard for fair treatment in the military.

Back home in the Bronx on April 15, 1991, Powell throws out the first ball of the new baseball season during opening day ceremonies at Yankee Stadium. "The real story," he has said of his rise from the streets of the South Bronx to the top of the military, "is that yes, I climbed, and I climbed well, and I climbed hard, and I climbed over the cliff, but always on the backs and the contributions of those who went before me. And your challenge, and my challenge is to tell our young people throughout the land, black, white, whatever coloration, that they've got to prepare themselves, they've got to be ready."

But rather than dwell on America's history of racism, Powell has elected to focus in his numerous public statements on the many opportunities the nation offers. "As much as I have been disappointed in my lifetime that we didn't move as fast as we might have, or that we still have forms of institutional racism, we have an abiding faith in this country," he said to the *Washington Times*. "Hurt? Yes. Disappointed? Yes. Losing faith or confidence in the nation? No."

As a result, Powell devotes as much of his packed schedule as possible to visiting schools and preaching his gospel of hard work. He tells black youths, "Don't let your blackness . . . be a problem to you. Let it be a problem to somebody else. . . . Don't use it as an excuse for your own shortcomings. If you work hard . . . success will come your way."

On April 15, 1991, the JCS chairman returned home to the Bronx, riding along the sweeping curve of his old block, Kelly Street, before arriving at Morris High School to speak to its current crop of students. Powell had not been back to the school since his 1954 graduation. "I remember the front door," he said to the assembly in a sentimental voice. "I remember the auditorium. I remember the feeling that you can't make it. But you can."

His tone rising, Powell encouraged the youngsters to avoid using drugs and to remain in school until they received their diplomas. Then, like a commander giving his troops their final instructions, he told the students: "Stick with it. I'm giving you an order. Stick with it." ✿

APPENDIX: AWARDS AND HONORS

The military awards and decorations and other honors bestowed on Colin Powell include the following:

Air Medal

Army Commendation Medal with two Oak Leaf Clusters

Bronze Star Medal

Congressional Gold Medal

Defense Distinguished Service Medal with two Oak Leaf Clusters

Defense Superior Service Medal

Distinguished Service Medal, U.S. Army

Joint Service Commendation Medal

Legion of Merit with Oak Leaf Cluster

Presidential Medal of Freedom

President's Citizens Medal

Purple Heart

Secretary of Energy Distinguished Service Medal

Secretary of State Distinguished Service Medal

Soldier's Medal

CHRONOLOGY

———— ✿ ————

1937   Born Colin Luther Powell on April 5 in the Harlem district of New York City

1940   Moves with his family to Hunts Point in the Bronx

1954   Graduates from Morris High School; enrolls in the City College of New York (CCNY); joins the U.S. Army Reserve Officers' Training Corps (ROTC) at CCNY

1958   Graduates from CCNY at the top of his ROTC class; commissioned as second lieutenant in the U.S. Army; attends Infantry Officers' Basic Training and Airborne and Ranger schools

1959   Serves as platoon leader and rifle company commander in West Germany

1960   Becomes battalion adjutant at Fort Devens, Massachusetts

1962   Marries Alma Johnson; arrives in Vietnam to serve as adviser to an infantry battalion

1963   Son, Michael, is born; Powell is wounded in action in Vietnam and receives the Purple Heart

1964   Enrolls in the Command and General Staff College

1965   First daughter, Linda, is born

1968   Powell arrives in Vietnam to serve as infantry battalion executive officer and assistant chief of staff, G-3, 23rd Infantry Division

1969   Enrolls in George Washington University (GWU)

1970   Promoted to lieutenant colonel

1971   Earns a Master of Business Administration degree from GWU; second daughter, Annemarie, is born

1972   Powell is selected as White House Fellow; serves as special assistant to the deputy director of the Office of Management and Budget (OMB); promoted to major

1973   Assumes command of the First Battalion, 32nd Infantry in South Korea

1974   Becomes operations research analyst in the office of the assistant defense secretary

1975   Enrolls in the National War College

1976   Assumes command of the Second Brigade, 101st Airborne Division at Fort Campbell, Kentucky; graduates with distinction from the National War College

1977   Serves in the Intermediate Office of the secretary of defense and as senior military assistant to the deputy secretary of defense

1979   Serves as executive assistant to the secretary of energy; promoted to brigadier general

1981   Becomes assistant commander for Operations and Training, Fourth Infantry Division at Fort Carson, Colorado

1983   Serves as deputy commander at Fort Leavenworth, Kansas; becomes senior military assistant to the secretary of defense

1986   Assumes command of the U.S. Army V Corps in Frankfurt, West Germany; testifies before the Tower Commission about role in the Iran-contra affair

1987   Becomes deputy national security adviser and national security adviser

1989   Promoted to four-star general; named commander in chief of the U.S. Forces Command at Fort McPherson in Atlanta, Georgia; becomes chairman of the Joint Chiefs of Staff (JCS); directs an invasion of Panama to apprehend General Manuel Noriega

1990   Directs the Operation Desert Shield campaign in the Middle East

1991   Oversees successful U.S. effort in the Persian Gulf war; accepts a second term as JCS chairman

FURTHER READING

Adler, Bill. *The Generals: The New American Heroes.* New York: Avon Books, 1991.

Binkin, Martin, and Mark J. Eitelberg. *Blacks in the Military.* Washington, DC: Brookings Institution, 1982.

Dalfiume, Richard M. *Desegregation of the United States Armed Forces: Fighting on Two Fronts, 1939–1953.* Columbia: University of Missouri Press, 1969.

Davis, Benjamin O., Jr. *Benjamin O. Davis, Jr., American: An Autobiography.* Washington, DC: Smithsonian Institution, 1991.

Fletcher, Marvin E. *America's First Black General.* Lawrence: University Press of Kansas, 1989.

Fowler, Arlen. *The Black Infantry in the West, 1869–1891.* Westport, CT: Greenwood Press, 1971.

Leckie, William H. *The Buffalo Soldiers: A Narrative of the Negro Cavalry in the West.* Norman: University of Oklahoma Press, 1985.

Morris, M. E. H. *Norman Schwarzkopf: Road to Triumph.* New York: St. Martin's Press, 1991.

Motley, Mary. *The Invisible Soldiers: The Experience of the Black Soldier, World War II.* Detroit: Wayne State University Press, 1987.

Nalty, Bernard C. *Strength for the Fight.* New York: Free Press, 1986.

Prados, John. *Keepers of the Keys: A History of the National Security Council from Truman to Bush.* New York: Morrow, 1991.

Smith, Graham. *When Jim Crow Met John Bull: Black American Soldiers in World War II in Britain.* New York: St. Martin's Press, 1988.

Woodward, Bob. *The Commanders.* New York: Simon & Schuster, 1991.

INDEX

PICTURE CREDITS

———— ❦ ————

WARREN BROWN, a native of Texas, is a freelance writer currently living in Cincinnati, Ohio. He has written several books for young adults, including biographies of Roald Amundsen and Robert E. Lee.

NATHAN IRVIN HUGGINS, one of America's leading scholars in the field of black studies, helped select the titles for the BLACK AMERICANS OF ACHIEVEMENT series, for which he also served as senior consulting editor. He was the W.E.B. Du Bois Professor of History and of Afro-American Studies at Harvard University and the director of the W.E.B. Du Bois Institute for Afro-American Research at Harvard. He received his doctorate from Harvard in 1962 and returned there as a professor in 1980 after teaching at Columbia University, the University of Massachusetts, Lake Forest College, and the California State University, Long Beach. He was the author of four books and dozens of articles, including *Black Odyssey: The Afro-American Ordeal in Slavery*, *The Harlem Renaissance*, and *Slave and Citizen: The Life of Frederick Douglass*, and was associated with the Children's Television Workshop, National Public Radio, the Boston Athenaeum, the Museum of Afro-American History, the Howard Thurman Educational Trust, and Upward Bound. Professor Huggins died in 1989, at the age of 62, in Cambridge, Massachusetts.